CHANGES OF HEART
Reflections on Women's Independence

Liz Heron was born and educated in Glasgow. She is a free-lance writer, translator and editor with numerous articles and reviews appearing in a large number of publications. Her book, *Truth, Dare or Promise – Girls Growing up in the Fifties*, was published by Virago in 1985, to great acclaim.

CHANGES OF HEART
Reflections on Women's Independence

Liz Heron

London and New York

First published in 1986 by
Pandora Press (Routledge & Kegan Paul plc)
11 New Fetter Lane, London EC4P 4EE

Published in the USA by
Pandora Press (Routledge & Kegan Paul Inc.)
in association with Methuen Inc.
29 West 35th Street, New York, NY 10001

Phototypeset in Linotron Sabon, 10 on 12pt
by Input Typesetting Ltd, London
and printed in Great Britain
by The Guernsey Press Co. Ltd
Guernsey, Channel Islands

Library of Congress Cataloging in Publication Data

Heron, Liz, 1947–
Changes of heart.
Bibliography: p.
1. Feminism—United States—Case studies.
2. Women—United States—Case studies. I. Title.
HQ1426.H456 1986   305.4'2'0973   86–5060

British Library CIP Data also available
ISBN 0–86358–028–9

CONTENTS

Introduction   1

1 A room of one's own   7
 Barbara Grant

2 The balance of happiness   25
 Ruth Bailey
 Madeleine Joyce
 Jenny Wilmott
 Julie Menéndez

3 Leaving home   79

4 The princess and the showgirl: femininity at stake?   113

5 Living together   133
 Joanna Watt
 Claire Booth
 Yvonne Hughes

6 Ariadne's thread   163

7 Motherhood . . . to have or have not?   177
 Claire Booth
 Joanna Watt
 Joan Rodney

8 Flying   219

Notes   237

INTRODUCTION

What do women want? This insistent modern question only scatters into a thousand others at every attempt to answer it. As women have become more and more the ones doing the asking – the subjects of the inquiry – a new, equally clamorous question arises: what have women gained?

The meanings of what it is to be a woman have been coloured by significant new perceptions; through their own struggles women have been the agents of these changes. Because of this women as a sex are now presumed to want a lot more than they ever did, not because they *have* less, but because of their consciousness of what they *can* have. And they are now presumed to have the wherewithal to get it.

The right to think, speak and act for ourselves; independence, autonomy – these claims are superficially taken for granted as met. It's no longer the arguments against female equality that we have to contend with, it's the careless assumption that we've got it.

This book isn't a history or a survey. It aims to suggest something of how women are living inside the realities of these new ideas, and how they survive the difficulties of living up to them, when soaring aspirations are often pulled back by circumstances or by the obstinacy of the past.

My approach has been personal and, obliquely, grounded in my personal history, because I've often taken my own history as a starting point for reflections on some of the difficulties that continue to harry and vex women in their efforts to change. Many of these difficulties emerge in relation to men, and in the dilemmas of relationships with men or of women not having them when they want to have them. I certainly don't assume that these are dilemmas common to all women, thereby overlooking the experience of lesbian women. I find it increasingly hard to generalise about women at all, and it seems that the best way to look at what women have in common is to start from individual lives and histories with all their particularities and differences.

Holding that focus has meant that the women whose accounts appear in the interviews here belong largely to my generation; they've traversed similar cycles of social change, and the women's movement has impinged on their lives with a broadly shared chronology, although by no means with identical effects.

The most salient themes are those of conflict and ambivalence; of reconciling emotional needs for an intimate, loving relationship with the desire for separateness and self-reliance; and of unravelling the knots created when the claims of others become entangled with the demands of the self.

Our potential for change in the present is always influenced by the enduring effects of the past and our often contradictory attachments to precisely those existing realities that we want to leave behind. Ideas of a better future sustain us, but if their promise fades, the balance of imaginative possibilities may alter in favour of a compromise with common sense: settling for things as they are because the alternatives carry too high a cost. When times are hard (and these are times of great hardship for many), the little deceptions of common sense close in.

Yet the changes affecting women have been too great and too numerous just to slip through our fingers now. These have become the context of our daily lives, and even of common sense itself. The future has already acted on the present.

If we're alive and attentive to our contradictions, perhaps we'll be less discouraged by the difficulties, less convinced that we're failing to match the expectations set up by the chimera of the new superwoman whose emotional vulnerability never betrays her, whose bank account never shrinks, whose life is one long rhapsody of glamour and achievement. We can be dwarfed by the glossy, inflated images of feminine success remodelled for consumerism as much as we risk unknowingly measuring ourselves by the standards of others that overlook or undervalue us.

Consciousness raising, then later women's therapy and psychoanalysis, and a growing body of scholarship and literary explorations, both fictional and non-fictional, have illuminated the role of memory and personal history in how identity is shaped and re-shaped. All of these have contributed to the process of change, and at the same time have helped us to understand that its progress also demands a constant reckoning with personal strengths and weaknesses, and with unresolved desires, as well as with the enormous inequalities of sex and class and race that still persist. When I ask what independence means to women I imagine it not as freedom from all this, for that's a shadowy ideal, but as the ways and means of transforming some of the stubborn realities of everyday life, and of creating new possibilities for ourselves.

CHAPTER 1

A ROOM OF ONE'S OWN

. . .when I ask you to earn money and have a room of your own, I am asking you to live in the presence of reality, an invigorating life, it would appear, whether one can impart it or not. Virginia Woolf, *A Room of One's Own, 1929*

Virginia Woolf addressed these words to an audience of young Cambridge women students in October 1928. I try to picture her listeners and see them tall, almost uniformed in sombre colours, all wearing hats, dark cloches or head-hugging helmets; earnest and attentive bluestockings, the daughters of lawyers and doctors, teachers and comfortably off tradespeople. Their Oxbridge world doesn't have the glittering decadence of *Brideshead Revisited*; I imagine their style a dowdy shadow of the period's enervated elegance: the reed-thin socialite in pale satins and jet-black brilliantined hair. Sitting in that lecture hall, notebooks in their laps, feet sensibly shod and firmly planted on the ground, these are serious women.

Such is my mental snapshot of that distant gathering. Who knows what were the individual dramas of these young women's lives, in 1928, two years after the General Strike and one year before the Wall Street Crash that toppled the world into the Depression. That audience off-stage but significantly present in Virginia Woolf's now classic feminist polemic is remote from my own history. What was my mother doing in 1928? My aunts? And I remember that my mother, aged 19, and her younger sister were both working as machinists in a Glasgow shirt factory, and their Oxbridge contemporaries basked in privilege by comparison. Two different worlds that wouldn't meet for decades, worlds etched with *them* and *us*.

But in another way, they do enter a part of my history. The struggles of the suffragettes before the First World War had finally and belatedly been vindicated in June of that same year, when the Bill giving equal voting rights to all men and women received Royal Assent. Virginia Woolf's audience were the first generation of fully enfranchised young women. In 1929 women of 21 would go to the polls for the first time, reaping the benefits of those early feminist struggles that had been organised around the demand 'Votes for Women' soon after the new century had dawned. Of course by then the vote had become the singular outcome of those struggles, while in reality it had been no more than the means to a much more important end: women's liberation. But that was something that was only remembered when, in the early 1970s, the contemporary women's liberation movement sent women looking for the legacy of the past.

It seems a long leap from then to now, across all those years of change. We can measure change in different ways: by changes in the law, by statistics, by scientific innovation, by the map of social policy redrawn from year to year. History in this sense is the outline of our lives. We invent and build what we can inside it, pushing through its limits with individual and collective action.

If we have come a long way since the early part of the twentieth century, we are still facing many of the same conflicts that women did then; we are still torn between the world outside the home and the conviction, that pulls us like a magnet deep in the psyche, that the true female identity resides inside the home's four walls, that it depends on a domestic lifeline and the claims of others for its substance. The difference is, of course, that the vision of choice and of other possibilities is now available to many more women than it was then – the choice, that is, not between unpaid and paid drudgery, but between domesticity and a separate identity that in some senses satisfies and fulfils. Though the painful conflicts persist, there is now more room for manoeuvre.

The subject of Virginia Woolf's book *A Room of One's Own* is the status of the woman writer, and the limitations imposed on her creativity in a world where the female intellect is devalued and women are materially worse off than men.

But the book's themes arch wider than this. The recommendation to earn money and have a room of one's own is made not just to aspiring writers, but to women who aspire to independence. Hence the clarion resonance of the book's title.

As well as existing as a space for writerly creativity, a room of one's own can be any space for self-reflection, self-awareness, self-recognition. Not just literally a room, but *room* to nurture and develop the inner world of consciousness and experience. In this sense it is a symbolic evocation of the physical and intellectual space which it is often so difficult for women to call their own.

Popular belief credits women with having greater access than men to their inner thoughts and feelings: 'feminine intuition'. Perhaps this is because women must rely more than men on interior sources of strength and affirmation. For if by historical insistence a woman's place is in the home, it has not been true that the home is there to provide those things for the woman in it. Woman *is* home, in the sense that she dwells there as one of its attributes, the core of its essence as a source of emotional and material sustenance for man, a refuge from the demands of the world.

> . . . and Jean turned back to the stove, always; she stood by the stove, the kitchen cabinets, the sink, the whole house moored to earth by her solid stance, just as the world outside went with Mitch in the car. He carried the world in and out in the deep khaki pockets of his workman's pants.[1]

The house offers a common and readily understood metaphor for contentment of heart and wholeness of spirit. It vouchsafes a sanctuary where the true self is inviolate. The English thatched cottage with its hollyhocks and honeysuckle figures as a motif initially in nineteenth-century literature that idealised pre-industrial rural society, and is pictured as man's place of refuge and solace from the sphere of production outside it; in it the family, divided by the industrial separation of home and work, has its balance and unity symbolically restored. That same sweet old cottage later reappears in a number of Hollywood melodramas made during the Second World War, when the traditional family circle was broken by male absence and women's departure for productive labour. The home as haven belongs to man, just as the public domain is his too.

In a public debate with the Conservative MP Duff Cooper on the question 'Is Woman's Place the Home?', Rebecca West in 1925 observed that 'when people say woman's place is at home they really mean that the home is a symbol of a state of resignation to the male will'.[2] In the sixty years that have elapsed since then, women as a sex have altered the sexual topography of economic production by leaving the home for work outside it in ever larger numbers, but domestic seclusion still implies conjugal hierarchies. This has made it hard for women to know where exactly they belong in their own right, what space belongs to them. Where has there been but to go inwards? Schooled in sensibility, destined to nurture and be attuned to the emotional needs of others, women, as a consequence, have developed the greater capacity for grappling with emotional confusion. But if they have learned to give rather than to expect emotional sustenance, perhaps their store of insight into feeling equips them better to weather loss or deprivation.

These are of course tendencies, not absolute psychological divisions between women and men. The archaeology of such differences is to be found in history and social structures; psychic structures, the basis for our perceptions of ourselves in the world and for our inner landscapes, are formed by both, as well as by individual childhood relationships and experiences.

The image of women as existing not for themselves, but for others – for children, for husbands, for infirm parents – may seem an anachronism in these days of enlightened social thinking and progressive public rhetoric, and beside women's increasing visibility and achievement in a large number of professional areas. But whatever relative headway women have made in the world outside the home, their progress is repeatedly halted and undermined by practical obstacles. More insidiously, self-image is touched by the lingering phantoms of the angel in the house, the self-sacrificing mother, the piously dutiful daughter, the outcast spinster and other baleful icons, whom we should be convinced were truly banished to the other side of the doors leading back to our Victorian past were they not so subtly but tenaciously present in many of the social rituals and cultural meanings that mark out women's place in the family and in the couple.

Women, rather than men, still emerge as the carers, tied to the kitchen, to domestic tasks and everyday family responsibilities, whatever their status in the job market. What underlies this notion of serving and soothing others, whether with food, clean laundry, or kind words and a well made-up face, is the idea that women do not wholly belong to themselves; they are an extension of others' needs and demands, and must continually surrender a part of themselves to please others.

So deeply ingrained are these cultural expectations that they override the logic of practical realities. Why do women so often accept as theirs the double burden of full-time employment and housework, shopping and cooking, with only some 'help' from husbands for the latter? Guilt and the buried meanings invested in traditional family roles come into play: a sense of female duty perhaps, or the nagging doubt that a woman's true worth depends on the caring tasks she performs for her family.

To resist the pervasive demand that they make themselves

available to others, women need some space for self-recognition. Betty Friedan identified the malaise of American middle-class housewives in the 1950s as 'the problem that had no name', and naming is the first step to claiming a separate identity, using words to describe the self-consciousness that is necessary to acquire some distance on one's situation. Writing has for a long time fulfilled the function of creating a space for women – a room in their heads. The domestic or romantic fiction, the confessional novel, the intimate diary have issued from the daily circumstances of life for women of a certain class and in certain periods. They have often come from the emotional centre of women's concerns in the home. Unlike other literary forms that demand long stretches of concentration, their production can, with an effort, be accommodated within the time allowed by domestic routines, whether by the nineteenth-century daughter of the leisured classes, forcibly occupied with trivial social obligations and genteel household tasks, or the twentieth century housewife and mother.

Writing is a solitary pursuit, but its social context has allowed recent generations of women writers to feel less isolated. A large number who have now made it their livelihood began writing in women's groups or for feminist publications. I now earn my living from writing, but had published nothing until the mid-1970s, when I was encouraged to contribute to *Spare Rib* and the paper of a community-based project I was involved in.

It is easy to see why the women's movement has produced so many writers. Not everybody can or wants to earn a living by writing. That isn't the point. The point is that the impulse that has moved so many women to write is very like the impulse that has brought women together and given them the space to think about themselves and their lives. Being able to satisfy that impulse is the nub of an independent identity.

In the late 1960s and throughout the 1970s, this impulse was asserted in the formation of consciousness-raising groups, as women, predominantly young, middle-class women with the benefits of further education and the leisure time to take such a step, propelled feminism once again into the forefront of political and social activism. It goes on being asserted in the 1980s, and the access to that kind of space and discussion has increased.

In *Women On the Line*,[3] published in 1982, Ruth Cavendish described her experience of working on a factory assembly line a few years earlier. She had taken the job for both personal and political reasons. She wanted to acquire a grasp of everyday working life in a factory at first hand, and come to grips with some of the realities of working-class women's experience that she felt needed urgent political attention. There is nothing dull or dry about her account of this experience and of the lives of the women she worked with. She does not underestimate their perceptions of themselves, and brings them to life with a vividness that goes well beyond the one-dimensionality with which working-class life is sometimes depicted by outsiders. But at the end of six months she is fully aware of the circumstances that severely restrict her fellow-workers' capacity to make room for the deep personal changes that the women's movement had envisaged.

> Working in the factory dominated the rest of my life. I was so tired and had so little time that I needed the weekend to recuperate. I had little energy to go to meetings in the evening and was quickly irritated if they took more time than necessary or were conducted in an unbusiness-like way. There was no way I could keep up with my previous network of friends. Working permanently somewhere like UMEC would entail a complete change in my lifestyle – less free time, more regular domestic routine, and more centred on a smaller number of close friends.
>   . . . The reason we haven't attracted working-class women to the women's movement is not that they aren't

feminist or are unaware. Our discussions are too up in the air for them and reflect a very different way of life. When you do hard physical work for eight hours and housework on top, you aren't inclined to go to meetings in the evening – especially with people you don't know and about campaigns that may not come to fruition for years. Unless it changes drastically the women's movement may remain primarily a movement of middle-class women and a servicing organisation for working-class women agitating for facilities that will benefit them, but without their active participation.

The signs are that even in the short time since these words were written, the scope for a greater number of women to think about political change has broadened. The growth in women's studies courses, ranging from the formal series of talks on aspects of women's history, literature, anthropology or psychoanalysis to the informal gathering that might have started as a one o'clock club for young mothers, has given many more women the framework for similar explorations. The late 1970s saw the development of Second Chance courses and New Opportunities courses, designed to help women build the confidence to return to paid work or study after caring for young children. An increasing number of women's networks and support groups have brought women together over a single issue, like tenant's rights, nuclear disarmament and the 1984–85 miners' strike, opening up new possibilities and new kinds of confidence.

It is not surprising that after the first rush of confidence inspired by the discovery of a common identity, there comes the urge to write things down, to create a literature of affirmation and revelation by committing private insights to public knowledge. This initial act of bearing witness to experience has many historical precedents. In the 1960s and 1970s (and still in the 1980s) a heightened consciousness and the need to give expression to what is overlooked or disregarded have produced new kinds of writing – from women writers' groups, but also from black writers' groups and groups of community-based working-class writers. Writing in these contexts is a form of collective consciousness raising in which skills as well as insights are developed. This process has revitalised some of the earlier traditions of working-class education through which organisations like the Cooperative Women's Guild were instrumental in encouraging women to commit their daily lives and experiences to paper. Two well-known collections of guildswomen's letters and memoirs, *Maternity: Letters from Working Women* and *Life As We Have Known It*, have been reissued in the last ten years as a result of the birth of feminist presses. For the women whose testimonies are contained in these volumes it is clear that the struggle for intellectual self-development was inseparable from the political struggle – for maternity benefits and better health care, for education and the vote, for improvements in marital status, for a minimum wage. Virginia Woolf wrote an introduction to *Life As We Have Known It*, when it was first published in 1931. In it she recalls attending the Guild's National Congress in 1913 and the thoughts and feelings that were prompted by hearing Guild members from all over the country speak about their lives and their needs.

> All these questions . . . which matter so intensely to the people here, questions of sanitation and education and wages, this demand for an extra shilling, for another year at school, for eight hours instead of nine behind a counter or in a mill, leave me, in my own blood and bones, untouched. If every reform they demand was granted this very instant it would not touch one hair of my comfortable capitalistic head.

For her, and for the other middle-class visitors, the Congress had been both 'a revelation and a disillusionment', for it showed them the gap between their own aspirations and

those of the Guildswomen, who were asking for the means
of improving their lives to a level that they themselves already
took for granted.

It was only on reading the letters and accounts of their
lives that some of the Guildswomen had written and sent to
the Guild's General Secretary, Margaret Llewelyn Davies,
that Virginia Woolf came to realise the broader significance
of the women's demands and where they led in the political
scheme of things, and to appreciate what the Guild had meant
for working women: 'It gave them in the first place the rarest
of all possessions – a room where they could sit down and
think remote from boiling saucepans and crying children . . .'

At a literacy group in Hackney, east London, ten women sit
chatting round a long table in a draughty barn of a classroom.
Three are part-time tutors, the rest come one day a week to
the group, which is for women only. The class is informal,
seen by the tutors as a supportive setting where the women
might gain some confidence along with better literary skills.
In one corner of the room is a small table with a kettle and
mugs, teabags and coffee jars. Every so often end-of-lesson
pips intrude, followed by bursts of noise from the corridors
and playground, for the adult education centre is located in
a secondary school.

Discussion – of current events and of personal experience
– takes up a fair amount of class time. When I ask the group
about their own perceptions of independence, it's clear that
the issues of work and home, of having some money and
time to call their own, have already been aired here.

Some are married, some are single parents, separated or
divorced, some single without children. The age range is
from early thirties to fifties. The nature of the group, a local
authority adult education class for people who feel they want
some help with reading and writing (though it's primarily the
latter) means that the participants have little in the way of
formal educational qualifications. As a result their status on
the job market has always been low.

Linda is in her thirties.

'It's nice if you've got a job and some money. I'm married.
I've had quite a few jobs. Not what you'd call good jobs.
I've worked in kitchens. Not very good money. This
morning we were chatting about your husband expecting
you to do lots of things – administrative work – because
you're sitting at home twiddling your thumbs and there's
nothing to do. About two months ago I stopped taking
telephone calls. He's a builder, my husband. People ring
up who want things done. Of course he got so much used
to me being there all the time, he asked me where I was
if I wasn't. But he wasn't paying me, so I put a stop to
it. He's got a lot of work on at the moment. If I'm in
I'll take calls, but I don't like to have to stay in just in
case. He just took it naturally that I was in all the time,
so I should take the calls and everything, sort out the
jobs. I was just being taken for granted, really.

'I think it's the hours that you work and the money
that you get, especially if you're working off the cards,
for me it's just too little. I was in a job that you worked
from 9.00 to 4.00, and I was getting £20 a week for
that, five days a week, a couple of years ago. I did it
because I wanted to get money of my own, and I didn't
have to ask for it. I fitted it in with the kids going to
school.'

In her book *Double Identity*,[5] Sue Sharpe cites numerous
instances of the importance of paid work in women's lives,
of the sense of independence and self-worth they gain, even
from low-status, low-paid jobs, although she notes that toler-
ance to boring, badly paid work varies greatly, in relation
to women's age and domestic situation. Those who have
left the job market to have children find themselves with
even more limited prospects when they try to re-enter
it and may consider jobs they wouldn't have taken on
before. The financial gain may be tiny, but sometimes

it's seen as worth going to considerable lengths to achieve it, for the sake of what it means as a small measure of autonomy.

Linda again:

> 'We had a terrible row one day. My husband turned to
> me and said "You're too independent." . . . He'd rather
> I was at home. One time he just wouldn't let me get a
> job. He said there was no need. So I still went ahead,
> but I didn't tell him. I had a part-time job in a dry cleaners.
> He didn't know about it.'

In a 1980 survey of the Pepys Estate in south London, carried out by the Lewisham Women and Employment Project,[6] at least one of the 107 respondents interviewed kept the same secret: 'My husband used to sleep when he came home from work. He doesn't know I've got an evening job!' Boredom, loneliness and feelings of dependency were as significant as financial necessity in the decision many of the women made to work outside the home as well as inside. 'I love work. I didn't like it before I got married. It gave me my independence afterwards. Having a child made no difference,' said one. And another: 'I want to work, even more now. I want to get out of the house. I'd go mad here.' Yet all of those with jobs received little or no help with household chores. As the interviewers observed, 'Most men continue to expect women to meet their needs first and slot their own employment into gaps in the household routine.' And as Sue Sharpe also found in her study, the demands of childcare and the search for local part-time jobs pushed many women down to the bottom end of the labour market. Job histories showed that women who had started their (paid) working lives in an office in many cases worked as cleaners, kitchen workers and shop-workers after marriage and childcare, losing skill, status and earnings, for the sake of 'convenience'.

If such low-paid, menial jobs matter as a source of social contact and for their symbolic guarantee of independence as much as for the money they bring in, then for some women the gains involved are so minimal as to be negligible. In the group I talked to several were convinced that it's just not worth having a part-time job, particularly if you're a single parent, since the pay is so low. 'I'd rather spend the time getting some adult education.'

In many parts of the country, particularly in inner-city areas, the character of adult education has evolved in forms influenced by the growth in community education throughout the 1960s and 1970s, expanding its scope to engage directly with local concerns and very much affected by what was happening in the wider area of education: an emphasis on multicultural experience, on local history and community arts, creative writing, feminism and, in general, more liberal definitions of what was meant by education. At the same time, women's studies expanded as a discipline and often overlapped with these other new areas. But perhaps more significantly, it is the generation of young women who in the late 1960s and early 1970s came to the women's movement from a background of expanded higher education who are now the teaching generation in the colleges, community education centres and polytechnics, as well as in schools.

This isn't to say that all women teachers and lecturers would call themselves feminists, but at the same time a very large proportion of women educated in the 1960s and 1970s, and pursuing careers in education, have been affected by the ideas of the women's movement and reflect this to some extent in their attitudes. There is abundant evidence of this in the responses and initiatives made by women teachers in relation to curriculum changes and the content of courses and syllabuses, participation at conferences on issues around sex discrimination and equal opportunities, and activisim in the teaching unions. But it is probably most apparent at the level of community education, given its social and political basis.

I talked to one of the women from the group alone at her home.

Barbara GRANT was born in 1944. She came to Britain from Saint Lucia when she was 17 to train as a nurse, but soon decided that nursing wasn't for her. She is now divorced from her husband and lives with her three teenage children.

'There were twelve in my family. Everything was done for me. I was completely lost when I came here. I had older brothers here, but no sisters, then my elder sister came later. She was like a mother to me.

'I did sewing, some shop work, waitressing – until I started having children. Then I gave up work. I got married just before I was 21 and I was married for eighteen years. I think there was pressure, in a way, because when you're from 19 to 20, people, your relations and friends, are expecting you to have kids. They're looking forward so that you'll get married and things like that, so therefore, in a way to sort of please them, that is what really traps a lot of young people into marriage – because you think of your parents.

'Some girls they don't care, they just grow up with their own thing. But with me I think from the time I was young I didn't want to mess about with any boy until I had found the right person . . . the right person was my husband. He was Mr Right you know.

'My husband felt it hard when we split up. He was asking me to reconsider. But it was too late.

'He would always be at home, not a gallivanter. About five years before the divorce I could see things weren't going to be right. I didn't like him telling me what to do. Before I started doing anything I'd have to ask him:

Where have I been if I go out; he wants to know everything.

'It's not harder being a single parent. I looked after the kids anyway. It is hard financially, with social security, but I prefer my freedom.

'He left in the July and in September I joined the women's group at the college. He was a book-keeper, he did all the letters and wrote to the family. I was lost; I had no confidence to do any writing. There were the letters to the children's school and I had to do the bills and the social security things. When I got married I never felt my writing was good. He had very neat writing. I used to let him do everything for me and I would go down and down. At Christmas he would send all the cards out.

'From the time I go to the college I feel very confident in myself. I saw it in the paper. Without the class I'd be lost. I get a lot of encouragement.

'What I would like is a waitressing job, something in the catering trade, part-time, 9.00–3.00, so I'd be home when the kids get home from school. If I had a job that's the time I would feel on top of the world, and men can go . . . . Now I have to depend on social security. If I get a job it's me supporting my children.

'I think a couple should talk, should be able to talk, respect one another in what they say. With my husband I couldn't. I would tell him something and maybe it would be OK, but later he would turn his back on me. He was possessive, he would say it was because he loved me. Now I love my freedom. I would like a friend, but not to get married again, not that kind of commitment.

'It's one thing marriage, but there's the chance that the husband might think "she's my property" or she'd think "he's my property", but I think if two people just live together without marriage involved, I think it's best.'

CHAPTER 2

THE BALANCE OF HAPPINESS

*P*anic sets in every time I think about the move, and there's still three weeks to go. Everything in these two rooms is me, even what was there before I arrived: kitchen chairs, table, pine bed (the mattress I brought with me), mauve carpet that matches nothing else. Everything has a singular familiarity: the olive and cinammon striped divan spread that I bought in a Greek import shop in Goodge Street, with the nest of cushions against the wall so that the bed can double as a sofa; my secondhand rosewood desk, the small table by the filing cabinet, collapsible bookçases, things on the wall.

Living alone, four and a half years of it, coming to an end. Elation when I first moved in, after more than a year of temporariness; temporary flat-shares with half-hearted attempts at communal living; staying with friends who are already cramped; never having a room to myself or big enough to be lived in. My own flat meant freedom and space, somewhere to indulge the first stirrings of an inclination to settle down, after years of travel and impermanence. What better place to burrow roots than a basement, damp like any other basement without the afterthought of central heating and extra insulation; but airy in the summer, in the winter soon warmed with the gas fire turned up full blast.

As the heat built up I'd sit half-curled in the basket chair by the fire, reading on winter afternoons, or working at my desk by the window. Above it, beside the bookshelves, was a postcard in a small black frame, one of a set I'd found at the flea market in Paris, all dating from 1919 and the Salon of that year, all with messages on the back, from the same young woman to her fiancé. Each title is printed under the reproduction in French, German, English, Russian and Polish. This one is 'Waiting'. It shows a young woman posed by the open window of an elegant room, leaning on the balustrade and gazing pensively into the distance. What is she waiting for? To rephrase the question answers it: who is she waiting for? And why have I chosen this card to put on the wall in a place where I can see it every time I raise my head from my work? When I do, I find it ironic.

The back room is draughty and gloomy, the kitchen min-iscule. I live most of the time at the front, but safe from intruding eyes in the street, in the summer screened by the overhanging foliage of an old, spreading plane tree, in the winter by my closed shutters, as soon as the light goes and I switch on the lamps. The room's cosy: no bright lighting, darkish colours, and it has everything I need: a television, record player, radio, books. In my basement I am safe, secret, all by myself, all to myself, like a sybaritic hermit in a cave. I cope well with living alone, sometimes lonely, but life is busy enough, with friends in the area, outings, visits, people round to dinner. Sometimes I'm nervous at night, waking up and feeling vulnerable in the dark, with silence heavy around me, and creaks and rattles threatening it.

Nothing is worse than the weeks that follow the end of a relationship − one that mattered. But I had to matter more than someone else for it to go on. At first there are tears, then I pull myself together, and everyday life goes on as usual. It's not just me putting a face on it; I do have energy, I work, see friends, read, watch television, don't dwell on it. It's a matter of principle after all. Not to give in, not to feel rejected, not to feel like nothing, suddenly insignificant and reduced just because I'm not important enough to a man for him to put me first. But at night I begin to have bad dreams. I dream about being asleep, alone, then waking to hear the sounds of someone breaking into the flat, a man who'll do me harm. I wake from the dream, deeply anxious, sometimes breathing fast, sometimes screaming in fear. The dream is repeated, *night after night. In the day time I get on with life; I'm only troubled at night.*

The dream is no mystery to me. But that doesn't stop it. I can't gainsay what it means, even if I batter away at it with the righteousness forced out of tidy feminist conviction. I'm convinced this is not how things should be. But they are. Do I need a man to protect me, to keep me safe, to stand between me and the terrors of the world? He was never there at night anyway, but that made no difference, so long as he was there, in my life. Someone who gave me what I needed, what I'd been waiting for: shelter and intimacy, unconditional love. Without this I'm exposed to the worst that can happen.

It's as well that my room is like a womb, a dim, quiet place where I can withdraw, seal myself into days and nights of self-sufficiency. Gradually, the dreams go away.

A long time has passed since then. Since that panic. Now this, another panic, invades me. Merging and separation. Inside me there's a fearful, disappointed child to contend with; under control as far as life goes, mostly, but re-emerging in a crisis.

Four and a half years of living alone, so that it's become a way of life. Everything under control, my control. Tidy when I want it to be, untidy when I can't be bothered and the dishes pile up at the sink, the dust gathers. I eat what, when I want, invite whom I choose, stay at home, go out, stay out, all night if I fancy. I can switch on company, and switch it off. I can indulge my mood, whatever it is. I can be me, whatever that happens to be at any particular time, with minimal interference. A lot of the time I like these arrangements. I don't get lonely any more; I'm not the awkward single woman at the party any more; there's a couple I'm half of.

But now everything invested in this room will be rubbed out. Me with it. Am I a fool to give it up, by crossing the line that separates single independence from couple living? When all my possessions are taken out and piled in the removal van, I'll have nowhere to turn, but to somebody else, who'll be there all the time, day and night, from whom there will be no escape into the comfort of solitude. All I can think of at the moment is the prospect of leaving this. Home. My place. In here I was safe. I came to terms with being on my own.

The prospect of this departure filled me with excitement and pleasurable anticipation only a few weeks ago. Until it became real. A new flat, bigger, nicer, lots of light. Not alone any more. No more inconvenient to-ings and fro-ings from my flat to his; the cat waiting, hungry, if I've stayed away too long. Now there's a mortgage, and more furniture to be bought. Two can live cheaper than one they say.

I feel a terrible sense of loss approaching. That and a sense of present dread. What will happen to me now? I feel hollower and hollower, everything of substance seeping out of me, until I turn into what I most fear. Until I don't exist.

In the 1970s Hollywood brought us a cycle of films that placed the issue of female independence centre stage. 'Women's pictures' were nothing new, of course: in the 1930s, 1940s and early 1950s they were a staple category. Scores of films with strong female stars such as Bette Davis, Barbara Stanwyck and Joan Crawford attracted audiences to the box office in their millions. They were made, primarily, for women; in them the female characters and the actresses who played them overshadowed the male roles; and their subjects were the dramas of the feminine dilemma, in a variety of shapes and forms. Their domestic pivot was that of choice. Between marriage and career, between motherhood and career, between self-fulfilment and self-sacrifice, between the happiness of a love affair and the sanctity of someone else's marriage. Without fail in these melodramas women suffered, and learned that the very nature of their lives as women meant that one thing could only be secured at the cost of another. Loss and tragedy were the outcome in most cases. Women in their cinema seats wept in recognition.

The 'women's pictures' of the 1970s reinterpreted the feminine dilemma, allowing that a few decades of social change and the ferment of feminism had introduced new elements into the scenario of choice. Although these date from the mid-1970s, already by the start of the decade the issue of women going it alone had been tackled in *Alice Doesn't Live Here Any More* – with Ellen Burstyn transformed from housewife to single parent on the move and in search of work, after her husband is killed in an accident – and *Klute*, a psychological thriller in which Jane Fonda plays a New York call-girl whose tough façade belies her emotional confusion. Alice's problems are solved at the end of the film when she meets Kris Kristofferson, falls in love and settles down. Jane Fonda's Bree gradually learns about emotional commitment and how necessary it is, in the arms of Donald Sutherland, who also rescues her from death at the hands of a murderer, a man who preys on prostitutes. In *Comes a Horseman*, a modern western made a few years later, Fonda undergoes a strikingly similar psychological development, from hard-bitten self-reliance to emotional surrender. This time it's James Caan she learns to trust and who helps her in the battle against a hostile and violent patriarchal figure, a man older than the hero, just like the murderer in *Klute*.

Although the focus in these films was on female independence in modern terms, in each case it was undermined, in the first by *Alice*'s facile happy ending, and in the Fonda films by the authority invested in the male characters. It is only through their insights or tutelage that the heroine learns about her own emotions, and in particular about the self-destructiveness of her refusal to yield emotionally to a man. If *Alice* suggested that guts allied to charm and femininity would beat the toughest odds (being forced to make a new life from scratch half-way through your thirties), the two Fonda films were harsher lessons in the dangers of female presumption. It wasn't until a few years later that the experience of female independence was given a more celebratory treatment by Hollywood.

An Unmarried Woman matched the temper of its times as

far as glossy *Cosmopolitan*-style versions of female independence went. Jill Clayburgh's husband leaves her for a younger woman and the film charts her progress through single parenthood and the New York social scene, from the miseries of rejection and loneliness to the satisfactions of a new life and new confidence. There's a women's group in the background, though its other members are somewhat less glamorous than the Clayburgh character; there are also several men in pursuit, and the heroine's sexy underwear gets some on-screen airings. In the end it's a love affair with Alan Bates's English painter which fully restores this woman's glowing sense of identity, although she does decide to keep the life she's built for herself rather than leave with him. The film's messages are ambiguous. Along with its reassurance that abandonment by a husband by no means spells curtains for a woman's (hetero)sexual and emotional life, there's the suggestion that it's really quite easy to face the world without a man and make it work, if you've got what it takes. Jill Clayburgh's heroine has: she's sexy, spirited and smart enough to give male creeps the comeuppance they deserve. She represents the triumph of the individual woman's new assertiveness. Although she's partnerless as the final credits roll, we're left in no doubt that things are going to work out, either with long distance love and Alan Bates, or another man waiting round the corner after one or two emotional ups and downs.

What's interesting about the film is this rather blithe celebration of achievement, which fitted with the idea, gaining media currency towards the end of the 1970s, that women had made it, that they had got what they wanted. With a superficial recognition of its claims, the women's movement could be rebutted and its continued existence identified as a form of extremism. The media myth that women have won the independence that was feminism's goal has put the onus on women. Even if we haven't swallowed it, it makes it harder to admit just how difficult it is to make independence a reality.

What makes it so hard is precisely the dynamic at the heart of so many of those earlier 'women's pictures': choice. Often wallowing in female masochism and ruthless in their implicit condemnations of female characters who dared expect to have everything, the films at the same time reminded their audience of how the domestic circumstances that led to these tragedies reflect the inescapable traps and dilemmas of feminine experience. They moralised but they also prompted women's sympathy for their protagonists' mistakes. Barbara Stanwyck sacrificing herself for her daughter's future in *Stella Dallas*, Joan Crawford losing out on all emotional fronts because she's built herself wealth and a career, in *Mildred Pearce*, and Bette Davis sacrificing her lover for the sake of his child in *Now Voyager*, all linger as the victims of circumstance and the cruel laws of an unfair world.

The emotional power of these heightened melodramas is intense because it reverberates in women's experience. Women are, after all, forced to make choices and reconcile splits throughout their lives. If in childhood the process of growing into a male or female identity is always governed by rejection or acceptance of particular kinds of behaviour, this is usually consciously perceived as something 'natural'; it's what is culturally taken for granted and operates at such deep levels that it is hardly noticed as choice. It is part of the business of becoming a girl or a boy in their social meanings. Of course while the 'essence' of femininity or masculinity can be reduced to a handful of neatly persuasive stereotypes, the variety of individual experience and of cultural and historical particularities means that the muddle of gender identity defies distinct patterns and rules. The emerging conflicts of adolescence may be heightened by the crisis of sexuality and the pressures that come to bear in favour of heterosexuality as opposed to more open sexuality or self-image.

For girls both the unconscious and conscious directions taken in the process of growing up are less a matter of choices than of exclusions. Our expectations become subtly defined as narrower than those of our male peers. While it is a child's spontaneous impulse to venture beyond the confines of adult space and adult boundaries and to escape adult authority, girls learn at an early age that it is often safer to stay close to home than to brave the unknown. They may still be adventurous in their play, but there is already a two-way pull being exerted. Home, marriage, motherhood come to enter the picture of imagined futures increasingly with adolescence, even if the dominant scenario in the foreground is something else: a job, a career, travel. How to reconcile the two assumes the character of a silent conundrum, with the half-knowledge that at some time something has got to give. There may be the option of procrastination, allowing work, travel and independent freedoms to be savoured until some time in the late twenties when it's time to settle down and have children. The future, and identity, are not only discontinuous, they are sundered: you have A, then you have B; you don't envisage both together, you are one thing, then another.

Already in adolescence our hazy, drifting images of the future are bounded by either/or, whether the choice is made sooner or later, and whether or not it has actual substance. Waking from the dreamy somnambulism of childhood, we face a world more starkly finite in what it offers. Yet for boys the anticipation of adulthood ignores such splits. Marriage and career aren't irreconcilable but complementary (and a young man on his way up may postpone marriage until he's safely on the career ladder, for financial reasons); becoming a father makes no difference to this equation.

When in adulthood we are confronted with the strictures of choice they are rarely as clear-cut as they once seemed, nor are they always quite the same choices that we foresaw. They don't end at the split between career and domesticity, which modern circumstances *seem* to soften into an easy choice. The whole question of whether to have children or not has repercussions that persist beyond the immediate decision. Children alter women's lives and present them with daily decisions to be made about what is best, so that the traditional burden of female responsibility for children continually tips the scales against a mother's own needs and choices. The very fact of biological time limits turns not having children into an act of irrevocable consequence, even where the decision is a passive one, since it assumes significance retrospectively, once the age of childbearing has been passed. What life offers us, it seems, can't be grasped with both hands – at least not without either great effort or relatively privileged circumstances. This is not only true for women, it has to be recognised, in a world built on inequalities of power and material wealth. But the patterns of female experience at their most familiar have a common thread – that one set of satisfactions involves the loss of another, that one kind of happiness rules out another.

Yet if women's lives are fraught with choices, these are now more than ever able to be reconciled in some ways. The newer women's pictures, while echoing some of the dilemmas of the past, do so with an eye to the future. In *The Turning Point*, made in 1978, Anne Bancroft and Shirley Maclaine play two friends entering middle age and discovering the bitterness of their regrets. For the one it is because her choice of a dancing career rather than commitment to a man or children now leaves her alone and without a future, for the other it is because dancing was ruled out by a pregnancy that forced her into early marriage and domesticity. The dancer sees herself replaced by younger women, her success at an end, the mother sees her daughter grow up and away from her and is faced with her own lost opportunities. Competition between the two women is centred on and then defused by the daughter's growing success as a dancer, and she comes to represent some future reconciliation of their separate choices in the past.

Other Hollywood films made at the end of the 1970s also touched on the deep divisions that are the product of women's different choices. In *Julia*, as in *The Turning Point*, the treatment is glossy and psychologically shallow. *Girlfriends*, a film made independently, was seized on by the mainstream distributors because of its currently fashionable theme, the friendship between two women, the one married, the other living alone and trying to make her way as a photographer. The difficulties of their respective situations and the resentments that, as a result, threaten their friendship are handled with humour, sensitivity and some suggestion of complexity.

Already, by the beginning of the 1980s, Hollywood had moved away from overt treatment of these themes. Women's independence and its dilemmas had been short-lived as a burning social issue (at least seen from a women's point of view – *Kramer v. Kramer* took on its effects in the life of a man and a child). At the same time, from the mid-1970s onwards there was an upsurge in women's participation in independent film-making, in Britain, in the United States and in Europe. Many of these films were made on shoe-string budgets, some were experimental in form as well as feminist in their themes, and distribution was limited often to festivals, cinema clubs and women's events. But a growing number of women directors have won wider audiences, although on the arthouse circuit rather than in the high street cinema chains.

One of these is the West German director Margarethe von Trotta. Her first feature film, *Sisters or The Balance of Happiness*, made in 1980, is the story of two sisters, Anna and Maria, who are mutually dependent but entirely different in personality. The story unfolds as a disturbing and haunting exploration of the splits in modern women's lives and identities. Maria is a high-powered secretary, successful, neat, cool and efficient. She succeeds in cutting herself off from emotion, and has little room in her life for relationships. The exception is with her younger sister. It was for Anna that she sacrificed earlier educational opportunities and went to work so that she could support them both and allow Anna subsequently to carry on with her studies. Anna herself is temperamentally at another extreme. Hypersensitive, melancholic, she is overwhelmed by her emotions and lives in an introverted state of quivering intensity. Where Maria is hard-working and apparently powerful in her attitude to the world outside herself, Anna is paralysed by her inner pain and her sense of dependency on her sister. Each sister is unbalanced, each is frustrated by the other, each is possessive and controlling with the other. Half-way through the film Anna succumbs to despair and kills herself.

Maria is stricken with guilt. From then on the film becomes surreal and dream-like. Maria sees Anna's ghost in the mirror, she cannot escape it, she is tormented by images of blood and suffering wherever she goes. Through friendship with Miriam, a young typist in her office, she finds some solace, but after giving her a home and offering to pay for her English lessons, Maria begins to dominate the younger girl and repeat the pattern of her stifling relationship with Anna. But Miriam resists, and will neither toe the line nor give up her own dreams. Neither a Maria nor an Anna, she represents a freer and less troubled spirit than either.

In its delineation of the relationship between the two sisters, the film cuts deep into the heart of the splits in female identity, the inner oppositions that are so hard to reconcile. Anna and Maria are two sides of the same woman, but unable to be integrated, and each undermining the other.

We swing one way, and then the other. If a woman is to take complete control of her life, if she is to be self-reliant and independent, deriving her satisfactions from her work, and taking no risks with relationships because they might overwhelm her, then it seems she must deny the expectations that formed her from birth: the expectation that safety and love would be hers so long as she gave up a part of herself.

It is hard to be resolute. It is hard to be alone, and if not quite alone still putting a distance between oneself and the other. It is so hard to do this that what we fear most – our vulnerability – is sometimes the only refuge. How do we achieve the balance of happiness, the balance of strength and vulnerability, of independence and dependency?

A feminist therapist who has run workshop groups for women alone for a number of years put it like this:

'It is women on their own who are the needy ones. Because they're so frightened of their needs they feel that these would overwhelm the other person and that there would be nothing left of themselves if they became that dependent. Women who would pride themselves on not asking for things, on not asking for help, are showing signs of neediness just as much as the opposite.'

For women who have developed a sense of autonomy, of independence in relation to work, friendships and other areas of life, who have constructed a life that is satisfying and by no means lonely, there can still be emotional gaps. Yet why do so many women express a fear of opening themselves to relationships whose intimacy might give them what they need?

In the accounts that follow four women express those fears, though in different ways. Each expresses ambivalence and a sense of her own emotional fragility. Each is afraid of being swamped and overwhelmed by feelings of need and vulnerability, of losing her separateness and being invaded by a man.

R UTH BAILEY   Ruth is 39 and a single parent. She has a teenage son who has lived with her ever since she separated from his father in his early childhood, although he spends a lot of time with his father and shares a close relationship with him. Ruth earns her living as a writer and teacher.

'At the end of 1969 I was a housewife and mother living in Leeds. I couldn't get Paul into nursery. He was 2 then. There was a women's group that had been going a few months. My friend said, "You must come," because she knew I had read Simone de Beauvoir and hated being a housewife. One day I did pluck up the courage to go, and I found it quite wonderful.

'I was aware I was hemmed in, but I felt a failure, I just felt depressed and guilty because I felt I should be able to use all my time and I should be liking it.

'I had no immediate prospects of financial independence. But in terms of working out independence of *mind*, taking independent action, I did. I was dependent on the nursery situation, which was dire, and the job situation, which was also dire. Jobs for women in Leeds were terrible, and I applied for things I was vastly overqualified for (I had a degree) and ended with a job in a factory making gas fires. I did it because of isolation. Because of moving to a new city and having a baby straight away, I was particularly motivated to get involved in things.

'What's changed for me since then is that I realise I can't psychologically stand being dependent on a man economically, because of all the awful things it brings up in the relationship, and how you feel guilty and as if you've got no rights to tell somebody where to get off. That's how I always felt when I was in that position.

'I've never wanted being a mother to be central. I think middle-class parents fuss too much about their children, organise things for them too much. I think I always have been dependent on my son, and I haven't recognised it until quite recently. It was when he went away to spend a term with his father that I had a breakdown a few years ago. More recently I know very well that I'm dependent on him, because I simply don't get as lonely. I feel really comforted just by his presence around when I feel bad. And by our routine. It is a very deep relationship really, and it's the feeling that he needs me, that there isn't anyone else that I can say that about as definitely. I know I'm really very dependent on that, although I do spend long times without him when he goes to his dad. I don't know how I would have stood it without Paul's bracing presence for so long. I really don't know how I would have stood it, not having anyone in the house to do things for, or who'll make you cups of tea. I think it would have been much worse.

'I think with a girl it would have been more difficult.

'When I had the breakdown I had been living in a sort of collective household. It was to do with not knowing how to depend on other people. I was taking too much weight and holding in too many things, trying to be autonomous and in a sense separate. I suppose I got made into a parent. It did reproduce family-type things in an unfortunate way, and we weren't really very conscious of it. I was very unconscious of anything to do with psychology then. I blundered on. I just reproduced the "toughie" and the person that other people would rely on. The sort of leader role. I had to crack up for it to change, and it's only years of therapy that have given me any way of tolerating my dependency needs. I suppose they must have been very refused from when I was very young. Too terrifying to feel, I pushed it all down. It eventually took its revenge.

'I always felt guilt and fears that I would be bothering my mother, that any need of mine would be a bother and a burden. And I think my father wanted me to be the boy in the family, and I put on an appearance of being much tougher than I was, and much more competent and boyish and brave and all these things. There wasn't really any place for a lot of needs and feelings. I'm sure that unconsciously it's all still kicking around. I know because when I meet my mother I get really really depressed. It's like the expectations are still sloshing around up against the reality.

'My relationships with men tended to compound what was there already. Like a really deep fear . . . . I just went from home to college to getting engaged and married; from the arms of one family into another. Then in 1971 I split up with my husband. But I was never on my own, I was never without somebody. From leaving home right up to 1976 I was with somebody. When one thing finished I just went out and got somebody else. It was very simple, I didn't question it, I just did it, and I don't even know if I chose the right people or anything. I don't feel as if I was choosing . . . I never considered being on my own. I never considered being without a guy.

'I had to have somebody – for intimacy. I wasn't really very intimate with women. I was just too reserved. It was only with men that you could get physical.

'I don't think I was particularly a parent figure in those relationships. Somehow it was my fault if the relationship wasn't working very well. I'd just get very confused and I'd feel like a bad child with daddy. I suppose I was in a way always thinking that I ought to be able to take the parent role with them and solve all the problems, and yet I couldn't, so I felt really useless. With men I so often feel that I'm going to be told off, that I'm somehow not going to be the person that they want, and that they're going to be sadistic. And they very often are. I didn't have a sense of knowing where you end and I begin. I couldn't really protect myself in a way.

'I still have a confusion in relationships, and a fear of men not somehow giving me the space that I want. I worry that they won't start trying to trim off your limbs . . . . But it's worth tackling that if there's enough excitement. I'd like to try living with somebody again, but I see that it would be trouble. I know it would take a lot of defining of myself and my boundaries. It would require a lot of negotiations, because otherwise it would just go back to the family thing and I would reproduce patterns. I can't conceive of anyone who would be committed enough, I can't conceive of me trusting anybody enough.

'It's not an aspiration of mine to live on my own and be independent. I was very scared of living on my own.

It's very limited. But once I started doing it, then it became quite exciting. I hadn't realised how very much space I'd actually needed, and had always been cramping myself in this communal situation, just feeling everyone's psyche crowding in. But at last I had all this space. But it did seem a *terrible* amount of space. It seemed really criminal to have so much space to yourself. Of course now it feels like a bloody shoebox. Now it's far less scary. It's addictive. I actually get ill if I don't spend enough time on my own, without the interference of anybody else. It's like something goes really wrong. I get tense. I feel ill.

'The bad things are loneliness, and feeling a failure. Because for a single person it's really hard not to feel a failure, in the way society is structured. I think feeling a failure is worse than loneliness, although that can be quite bad. The demoralising thing about it is that you don't matter. It's not that you're not a person who is worthwhile, and she achieves things; it's not that sort of lack of self-esteem. It's this feeling of not mattering in the world because you don't matter that fantastically much to any other one person. I think that's really hard. I've had to fight against that a lot. I do feel like an outsider. But yet I'm not, in terms of a lot of people that I know in the same situation, and a lot of people statistically.

'I think it's less social pressure on men, and yet it's worse for them, because they're usually much more narrow and directed in what they think they ought to have, and they're not flexible. So they're not able to fill their life with friends. Like one man friend of mine who's very fixated on the idea that you must have a proper relationship, and if you don't have that your life is a total misery. Whereas women – certainly women I know – are much more flexible about getting things that they need, or doing things that are pleasurable. The need is still there, though. And the social thing is really difficult. But I think it's much easier socially for a single man, just to go around and be accepted. And be chased by women. But for a single woman, certainly over a certain age, even if other people aren't thinking all sorts of things about you, you're thinking them about yourself. You're *thinking* that *they're* thinking, Why hasn't she got a man unless there's something really wrong with her . . . or frigid or really neurotic, or she's a real ball-breaker. There are lots of negative things attached to it. So when I'm on my own I'm trogging along and I can get quite unhappy, feel quite doomed about it, but I feel my *very worst* in social situations, because I start this awful thing of seeing paranoically through other people's eyes. So it just gets really impossible. I get trapped in this social refraction.

'One thing I do fear about being with men or maybe living with a man is that I'll not be as productive, because of their needs breaking in on your creative space. Even when they're not actually demanding anything you feel that you ought to be somehow intuiting what they might need, and fulfilling it.

'I think it has happened to me that if I'm with a man, and there might be something really difficult I have to do that involves going out in the world – which I'm not terrific at anyway – if there's somebody there I'll spend a lot of time sobbing and being miserable; it's been more difficult to go out into the world and do it. Whereas if I'm just on my own, I think, "Oh God, I really don't want to do this; it's awful." But I sort of push down the feelings and I do it. It's like if somebody is there you expect more help from them with your life. So you can be a little more passive than if there is nobody there. If you don't expect any help, you force yourself.

'Independence has actually never been an aspiration of mine. The word doesn't summon up any powerful emotional resonance. There are many ways of being distinct and being self-defining that aren't necessarily the same as independence. I didn't even want to have a career when I was young. I didn't think in terms of sensible things like you have to be financially independent and have a job. I just blocked that off. And all I wanted to be was an artist and I didn't care how I got the money for it. That's been the biggest drive in me, to get a self-definition that comes through creative work. Financial independence is very shaky still with me, feeling that I can definitely earn my living and support myself without support from the state; it's not really developed. I'm not your all-round wage-earning economic unit.

'In a certain way the women's movement has made it easier for women on their own. Intellectually, but emotionally no, because the women's movement can't change what you've inherited from childhood. It doesn't really change deep-seated things. It means that there is a practice of women being friends and women doing things together, which makes it much easier for your single woman who's part of feminism to survive, so it helps in ways of thinking about it, and also what you do with your day. Deep down it doesn't really attack and get at the source of it. And the feelings. Like my mother said, "You've got to have a good man to look after you," when of course you'd be the one looking after the good man. But that's never mentioned.'

Women alone must dispel a social image that presumes weakness and inadequacy, and turns the single woman into a rejected outsider. They must either retreat from it or push it away, and that distorting reflection enlarges the tender pressures of need: for intimacy, for the sharing of burdens and for proof that others need them. It is the tenacious idea of female vulnerability that increases a sense of needing protection – yet women's fears are repeatedly shown to be disproportionate to actual physical danger; violence against women is more of a reality in the context of marriage and the home than on the streets of a city late at night. It is the potent and pre-enacted idea of female passivity – the waiting-to-be-asked state of adolescence – asked to dance, to go on a date, to marry – that can give an undercurrent of doubt to behaviour that's active and powerful. It is also the sense that however strong, however capable and responsible a woman may be, there is something missing in her self-sufficiency, something unreachable beyond it, for we grew up learning that the ideal partner would be a man who was bigger, stronger, older and more powerful than ourselves.

Perhaps this is why the temptation to let men take over in the couple is so overwhelming; to give in to weakness, paralysed and infantilised by the knowledge that daddy is there, so he can take charge of things, grown-up things out in the world. Ruth Bailey's description of how she tackles daunting tasks on her own – ' "Oh God, I really don't want to do this; it's awful." But I sort of push down the feelings and I do it' – in contrast with the hopelessness and misery she's felt when in a couple, strikes uneasy chords of recognition. If we are seized up, immobilised by the fear of dealing with the world, every now and then, it's no mystery. *Get out there, be assertive*, say the behaviourists and the women's magazines. *Complain to those neighbours, go for that high-flying job, be a self-starter. You can do it.* You can. But the effort of pushing against the grain of what so strongly held you back in the first place can be quite a strain. What Colette Dowling called 'the Cinderella complex' in her best-selling book of that title – women's tendency to collapse into passivity when a man is around to lean on – is less the 'hidden fear of independence', the flaw in women's psychological make-up that she claims it is than an understandable urge to succumb to dependency precisely because independence is not made easy for women, and it is not built into the self-image we internalise from an early age.

Some days I think of the Sleeping Beauty. Fairy tales come in handy. Poor girl, there she was, happy and active, full of fun and curiosity; and as soon as the blood started to flow, all the excitement and adventure in life became but a distant, dream-like memory. Poor girl, dulled by the onset of woman-hood (a witch's curse, too) into waiting for a man, fast asleep, for years and years. Meanwhile, the forest outside got thicker and thornier by the minute; impassable for most princes that came that way, despite their swords and even, for the more determined, strong machetes. If they couldn't get in, she couldn't get out.

Some days I suffer from phone phobia. It's a mild form, and it only dates from the time when I stopped living on my own, and started living with M. I can answer the ringing, for it has to be silenced, though with hesitation; but the thought of lifting the receiver and dialling fills me with jittery anxiety. This doesn't happen when I work outside, in a busy office an hour's bus ride from home. When I'm here, however, alone at my desk, cut off from the teeming mass of the working world and its web of routines, my connection with it drops away. To break out of my solitary vacuum, to push myself purposefully towards it across the most tenuous route, the telephone line, seems to demand a formidable exertion. The pull of solitude is strong; I have to shake myself free of it and re-imagine my place in the world out there.

I become increasingly reluctant to use the telephone. Only with friends, people I know well, do I relax and forget my awkwardness. I am loath to make business calls of any kind: the bank, the building society, the shop where I've bought something delivered with missing parts. The same goes for personal appearances; returning faulty goods, making complaints, organising repairs. We make deals, M and I: if you ring the builders about the roof, I'll do the dishes; if you take the kettle back, I'll cook the dinner even though it's your turn. Some days I despair of ever coping with all the practical responsibilities of adulthood; I want someone to wave a wand and make it all all right. Some days I can't even face the corner shop. Some days it's a different story altogether. I can do anything. Leave home and fly across the world.

Agoraphobia is a neurotic symptom predominantly exhibited by women. A fear of open spaces. Women who suffer from it are afraid to go out, afraid to leave the house. It is a condition that reflects the actual pressures of domesticity: women confined to the small spaces of a flat day after day because of childcare may lose the will to go far. But it is also a symbolic reflection of the idea, implanted at an early age, that home is where women really belong, that this is where it's safer, that we are meant to abdicate responsibility for ourselves and leave it to men to go out into the world.

Women on their own have to deal with the world. There is no one else to do it for them. It can be enormously satisfying, and a source of pride and confidence, but it isn't easy. Whether a woman is alone because of circumstances or choice, through separation, divorce or widowhood, whether she has never lived in a relationship with a man although she has relationships with men, or is a lesbian living alone, there is always social pressure to contend with. The form it takes will vary, but in every case there's the lurking knowledge that our society looks askance at the unattached woman. The family is the norm, the couple is the norm; it is family life that appears to unify our society, shattering the barriers of class and wealth with a chain of images that stretch from the apex of the social hierarchy – the Royal Family – to its base. It is in family life that we are meant to recognise common experience with the rich and famous, the royal and the star. They are the kind of experiences that are the stuff of soap opera and tabloid journalism, and if we don't see ourselves in them then we are different. The family and the couple are where we are meant to share our worries and have them halved. Blood is thicker than water.

Because the world at large allows men the status of independence, of being in charge, the social mirror shows the man on his own a picture of strength rather than of weakness. This reflection is also founded on such material realities as men's greater spending power and greater mobility (in literal terms: far more men than women own cars; and in access to the places where it is socially more acceptable for a man to go on his own, like restaurants, clubs, pubs, and situations like parties). The prince, alone, hacking his way through the forest.

MADELEINE JOYCE

Madeleine Joyce is 32. She lives alone – her flat is rented through a housing association in which she has been active for several years. She works in an advice centre.

'I just find it a sort of mystifying, bemusing experience for me to be on my own. I think I do cope reasonably well.

'I had such a strange childhood and adolescence. I was an only child. And living in a quite isolated rural situation, I spent an awful lot of time on my own as a child. That's left me with a certain resilience about being on my own. I think other people who've had a very sociable childhood with very strong family or neighbourhood networks, find it harder. But that isn't to say there aren't a whole range of situations which being on my own I find very difficult: little sort of qualms, being a bit uncomfortable, a bit anxious, quite a range of emotions before going to a party or if I'm in social situations where the couple is very predominant and you feel very odd if you're not seen to be in one.

Marriage
'I was married. I got married when I was 22. I think the contradiction was a bit of what I was saying about childhood. One of the things about being an isolated child was being very shy – well, I always found it difficult to be in group situations, like parties. I'm quite socially inept. And also feeling a bit of an outsider, coming from a working-class background and going to the grammar

school and being with people whom I saw to be very articulate and very confident, children who were better off in all sorts of ways. I've always felt that one of the things that that led to was, in my late teens and early twenties, having relationships with men who I hid from the world behind. I maybe looked for and certainly responded to men who were much more extrovert than me, seemingly more competent in all sorts of things than I felt I was. And feeling very strongly that I wanted to be sort of looked after by them, and got through the world by them rather than having to deal with it myself. And I think that getting married was the high point of that kind of relationship really, because I saw it as a way of providing me with some security and some permanent way of dealing with the world. It feels very naive looking back on it now. It's always very hard looking at things retrospectively.

'What changed in lots of ways was, although in terms of historical time it could easily have been feminism, it wasn't actually feminism, but what made an awful lot of difference was starting to work and earn – stopping being a student – within a couple of years being forced into situations where I couldn't hide behind anybody. It was no good me pretending I could. The sort of day-to-day demands that I had to respond to of a job began to make me realise. It was still quite confusing, but it was certainly during that period of time that I began to realise that I *couldn't* depend on somebody else. I had to do some things on my own, and push myself into dealing with things. And within the relationship he had a job that meant he was working into the evenings; it was quite a demanding job, with not a lot of space for me. So even down to the very basic level of me coming home from work and expecting somebody to be there to make it all feel a bit better if I'd had a hard day, he wasn't actually there to do that. So I did have to become more reliant on my own company. I was a teacher then, for a year and a bit.

'In a way the things I've been saying don't actually reflect quite what happened at the end of it, because after about a year, I got involved with somebody else, and it wasn't really until after I left the man I was married to and moved out, that I did begin to realise. I suppose I realised that it was not just a case of me finding somebody different, but it was also about me really changing in all sorts of ways, and wanting different things.

Alone

'I wasn't at all involved in feminism, at that time. In some ways I felt relatively strong when I moved out, but about six months later I started to be overwhelmed by what I'd done, and felt lost and confused by it, upset by it. And feminism still wasn't very much – it doesn't feel like it was a major part of my life at all.

'Because I got very depressed about six months after I'd left the marriage I got referred by my GP to a psychiatrist and one of the things that we focused on quite a bit, because of all the things that had happened in that relationship and at other times, was that emotional withdrawal from a relationship made me sexually withdraw. I remember I bought *Our Bodies Ourselves* around that time and read that quite a lot and found it exciting because in terms of drawing support from women's groups or the theory of the women's movement there wasn't very much of that.

'What actually began to build my confidence in myself was active trade unionism. The job that I'd taken after teaching was just beginning to move towards developing trade union organisation. That proved to be something where I found confidence in myself.

'I haven't actually chosen to live with a lover since my marriage ended, although I've shared a house quite a lot of the time with other people, one of whom did become a lover. In the two years after leaving the marriage I struggled a lot with the idea of being independent and living on my own, and, for quite some time after that – I think for a long time – I sort of over-reacted to what I saw had been this very unrealistic dependence on somebody, which I wasn't going to repeat. I wasn't going to expect somebody to save me from the world. What I feel now is that I very much over-reacted to it with certain things – like 'this is how I will maintain my independence and I will not become a couple again', which in retrospect I think led to very negative and destructive relationships that I did have.

'One of the things that was often quite a point of dispute was keeping friendships as something to be regarded as very important, so that I didn't become cut off in the same situation ever again, and keeping them very separate from any men that I did have a sexual relationship with. I had this rather strange division between people who I would tend to regard as friends and would spend time with and put quite a lot of energy into, but who remained over here, while the men I had sexual relationships with were over there. I decided that made me feel better.

The jigsaw

'I don't think that those needs to be looked after really went away. I'm more aware of that now. It's taken me the last couple of years to acknowledge that they do exist and that they are more difficult than I'd thought they were to deal with. I was quite ill during the middle of those first two years, and I was still feeling very needy around relationships, and I think I thought, "This is not how it *should* be." I saw it as a temporary problem that would be solved when I got better, and I would be stronger and independent. I'd still strive towards this vision of what that felt, of what it could be. I did have a very unreal expectation of my independence and strength. . . . Still feeling reasonably confident and strong in certain areas of my life, actually having a relationship with someone revealing all these chasms of being scared and being weak and fragile, and feeling very caught up in that – half the time feeling very angry with myself for being so fragile, and looking at it very negatively, and half the time wondering, "Is it really so unacceptable?" – and yet on the other hand feeling angry with him because he can't respond to them in a way that makes me feel better.

'Another thing is that having been open and wanted to build a particular relationship, it actually needs quite a lot of time and a lot of energy to do that in a way that makes any sense to me, which leaves me less time to spend with the friendships that I have been putting a lot of energy into, and that always made me feel stronger because I had them whatever else happened. The balance between work and the difficulties of work, and still wanting to keep these relationships here, and yet wanting to develop this sexual relationship, just seems like this puzzle – a sort of jigsaw puzzle. The pieces never quite fit because either I end up putting an awful lot of that energy into the relationship with him and feeling like diminishing the other things, or I opt out of putting energy into him to go back over here to those other things. I just never quite get it, the whole thing just constantly moves around, because different things mean so many different things.

'One of the things where I tend to be very angry, which may not be so justifiable, is that he seems to have this ability to box things off more, in a way that means that he moves from one situation to another without letting a lot of other things get entangled into it, so that while I experience things if I'm feeling unhappy about work, that sort of spills over into everything else. Or if I'm unhappy about that particular relationship or any other relationship, that spills over into my ability to handle work successfully. The lines all get very blurred, and so I get very stressed. He seems to have this ability to focus his energy. When he moves out of being in direct contact with me, whatever we're going through, I don't feel I'm such a negative drain on his energy and other bits of his life as he feels to me.

Children

'I've never been economically dependent on a man. I don't think I've ever wanted to be. I made a decision not to have children, quite clearly, so that isn't an option. I never ever felt any inclinations towards babies, or certainly towards giving birth. I never remember at any time feeling I wanted to have a baby, and although I've shifted a bit in terms of spending my time with children and enjoying that, really I've always been very worried by the thought of it – always feeling quite negative about the idea of that responsibility, of that sort of dependent person. I find it incredibly scary; watching close friends having children and seeing them adapt to that, but still feeling incapable of imagining myself doing it, imagining myself being responsible and adjusting myself to that extent. I don't think I quite still understsamd how I happen to feel like that, and yet I've always felt it.

'I suppose when I was a child and adolescent I must have expected I'd get married and have children, but I don't have a very clear memory of that. When I did get married I just didn't want to. Certainly one of the things I was always very adamant about was the idea of a baby – it seems to be the baby period that was particularly unacceptable. And so there was a sort of option about, well, maybe, I might think about adopting an older child. That somehow felt more possible, but the idea of actually giving birth and of looking after this person as a baby – my husband was quite accepting of that position, although he subsequently now has two children.

'In terms of independence I think it's always been my fear that I would lose everything – just of being taken over, totally.

The future

'I think I'm probably less clear about the issue of living or not living with a man than before. Just as I've felt shaken by what does happen to me in a very close relationship, I can't quite decide any more what I think about living together, in the sense of whether or not that's just a false division for me to make, and whether or not it's still something that I see as representing a mythical dependence more than it really is.

'It's difficult for me to be very clear about it as well, because of having moved very deliberately from a collective living situation about a year and a half ago, because I found I wanted more space. And that's coincided at the same time with this closer relationship with Tim. I don't feel quite yet very clear about it, because I still think in terms of the space, about it being *my* space, and all the time I can have there on my own. I can share that space with other people so it doesn't become totally involved with him, and yet on the other hand if he disappeared from my life tomorrow the *gap* that I would feel in my own home – even though we have kept a sort of physical distance – just because he does spend a lot of time with me there, would mean that I would still feel dreadfully alone in it. To break up would be just as significant as if we were living together. Although there is, I suppose, a stability and security in living separately, so that . . . well, I think what I'm trying to get at is just really my confusion about how I maintain my independence.

'There's been quite a big gap really in terms of feminism. Quite a lot of the time I feel some reassurance at least; if it's not necessarily progress, at least there is the reassurance of not feeling isolated. The reassurance is there, even though you're feeling a bit frustrated with the fact that those questions still exist. But I think what I still find is that that is still fairly fragile at some of the most difficult points in my relationships with men, and I can still be in a relationship with a man and feel very alone in it, at the time that I'm sitting in a room with him and there are these needs and difficulties and wants, and old issues between us really at a high pitch. I can still, at that point, feel very lost and very alone and slightly crazy, all sort of negative feelings.

'When I'm in the situation I tend not to see how men can be dependent on me, not because it doesn't exist. I just don't see it. I tend to see them being strong and independent and me being weak and dependent. But then if I have conversations with friends who know both Tim and I they'll point out to me sort of logically, on a rational level, that obviously what I'm saying isn't true. But the feelings are quite strong, that I see him as strong and independent. I can see things happening better in other people's relationships than in my own.

'I admit to quite a lot of my dependency with him. There's still a tendency to pull away, to be very defensive about it. It fluctuates, between pulling away and acknowledging it. It's one of the difficulties we have.'

To be on your own as a woman and feel right involves such an effort of conscious will, such a battle with inner uncertainties and fears and such a resistance to the force of social and cultural persuasions that women's ability to do so is testimony to remarkable emotional resources. But for many women this perhaps can only be done with the creation of a second skin that will hide vulnerability and ensure protection.

In a close relationship you can let go, you can allow yourself to be more needy and more vulnerable; but at the risk that the skin will peel away, the armour crack, leaving you exposed to more than you can bear.

It is as if women cannot be strong *and* dependent (by this I mean sharing a mutual dependency) at the same time. It is as if we see ourselves as having only two options: to go without the emotional sustenance we need or to collapse completely into total emotional dependency. To discard the defences that keep us whole, that contain us and our separateness, is to risk dissolving into someone else's identity. How to reconcile the strength and the dependency, the characters of Maria and Anna, is a problem at the heart of female psychic structures, formed as they are in a mesh of social and economic definitions that leave women little room for easy reconciliations.

We are either one thing or another; if we are two things, we are split between them. Men are less torn between dual identities, they manage them along separate tracks, and so perhaps find it less of a challenge to the imagination to move forward with confidence and assume new roles and responsibilities, or discard old ones. Like Madeleine's lover Tim, who has the 'ability to box things off', men have a greater capacity to slip with ease from one role into another, without undermining either, or to abandon one role for a new one without the panic of loss and doubt.

Such single-mindedness is something women have to strive for, and there's a particular kind of glamour in the self-assurance that goes with it, whatever insecurities it disguises – it inspires envy, attraction and irritation. It's the otherness in this aspect of masculine personality that makes it so fascinating; oddly, in those rare women who have it, it's infuriating, because so unclouded a sense of direction is often inseparable from a degree of insensitivity that we take for granted in men but find intolerable in women.

There's the fractured familiarity of Madeline's jigsaw, her feeling that the different bits of her life can't be made to fit; an absence of control, of integration; a need to smooth and match the edges of things, to close the gaps.

To reach a point where we can live alone and feel secure in our capacity to look after ourselves, without any hurtful sense of exclusion or inadequacy; or to live in the intimacy of a couple without feeling threatened or diminished in our sense of self, without drowning in symbiosis, would be to hold the fine balance of independence and dependence that seems so delicately necessary.

J ENNY WILMOTT 'My first big independent step was living with my boyfriend when I was at teacher training college. I was from a working-class background and there was a lot of pressure around from friends too – to wait, to get engaged, to get married. I was 20.

'Now it may have been that lots of women slept with men, but it certainly wasn't the kind of thing you'd say, and there was the big thing about having an engagement ring. I feel awful because most of my friends now had slept with men when they were 16. But it was quite an act of independence. It enabled me to become more political with very small steps. Living with this man, which my mother never knew; it was a very, very risky thing to do.

'At the beginning of the women's movement when I first read about living with a man, of course it was definitely not the thing to do. It was considered quite reactionary, and I remember being very upset. It had been such a big thing for me to have made the *first* step . . . . I knew that somehow I'd resisted the engagement ring, going back home . . . . My relationship with him was part of my achievements that I had done that.

'It was another kind of risk to let that go, and I didn't actually do it. I used to spend weekends with him in Birmingham, and the week in London. I'd drive back and about half-way on the M1 coming back to London I'd feel this incredible sense of liberation, but I didn't let him go. It was really weird. So I did it every week and I was totally split between being kind of independent in the week and starting this new life, this job I had got by myself, and then going back there at the weekends. I kept this up for a year. I liked living with him.'

Jenny has lived alone for the past four years. During that time she has had no serious involvements with a man, although she has had a few casual affairs. She has recently met someone with whom she is becoming quite deeply involved, which has made her consider some of her ambivalence.

'I do like living alone. I prefer it to living with others, because when I was living with other people I found it very difficult to articulate anything about what my needs were. I couldn't stand up for myself. I felt guilty all the time. I wanted some space . . . . The way I achieved that was by buying a flat, and it was quite wonderful. So far from being alone I actually felt just wonderful. So that living on my own took account of all those very, very good things.

'I didn't feel inadequate because I was on my own. It was less about living on my own and more about not being in a relationship. I felt a kind of desperate wanting, longing for somebody to be there. It was like a desire without an object really, and it felt just unbearable . . . .

'Well, there was this feeling that I thought I could manage. I wasn't managing all right on my own. It was a lot of stress. But on another level I was all right. Like I'd got the flat, my own home. I really believed it. But meeting Mike made me realise that all the certainties I thought I had weren't as certain as I thought they were, and that was very funny. One of the things about being independent was realising just how terribly empty this feeling was – which I had known was there, but I didn't do anything about it. Like sometimes when I would get home and there'd be nobody here, and not knowing how to deal with it, how to make the transition from coming

in to getting on with something, and thinking that I had
to . . . work. Not just relax.

'I think I wanted somebody to be here. I do have a lot
of friends, and yet it felt like there was this aching
emptiness that I hadn't wanted to look at. But then it was
equally frightening to start a relationship with a man
that mattered, because it felt like if I'd opened that up
then and looked at that it would be just like back to
dependency. That was what was so really frightening
about it. So at the same time as I actually wanted to
make this relationship happen I was absolutely petrified
of it continuing.

'Before, everybody ran away. That's the thing about
being independent. Given that you're independent and
live on your own, and given men, you're terribly kind of
together and powerful and they run a mile And partly
it was just the feeling that I just wasn't independent
enough.

'You see I managed to convince myself that I didn't
want anybody here, because I was so frightened. So I
was definitely into convincing myself that the last thing I
wanted ever was to live with anybody. I have come to
a recognition that I didn't need to live on my own, but I
was so petrified of the idea of living with a man, losing
the thing I'd fought so hard to get, which was
independence, that I thought I might have to give up the
flat and share a house. Live with a man? Good God No!
A little while ago a friend of mine came and told me she
was thinking of moving in with her boyfriend. I genuinely
didn't understand or I wouldn't face the prospect of
what was all right about her doing it. *And* I convinced
myself that I'd never want to live with anybody.

'People do say that over the past few years I've got
much more confidence. And living by myself has actually
been part of that process. So it was all that, the fact that
that was all such a struggle to build up, and the fear of
losing it. Mike stayed here for a couple of weeks and I

didn't know how to relate to him being here. Living with anyone would feel like giving up something.

'Living alone was the beginning of the development of my own academic work. The first time I lived with a man it was different. I didn't have friends, I didn't have the split. I didn't feel the same way – not wanting to be on my own in the same way. But work and achievement and my relationship with women friends became more and more important in defining the boundaries of myself. After having developed things about myself, to actually then go back, or what seems like going back, is scary. And that's how I felt in relation to Mike.

'Sometimes when I've felt particularly awful, like when I was feeling very lonely, I just felt like a weed. Like, you know, if I was stronger it would be OK. I don't really believe it, but that's what it felt like. I know it's crap actually.

'There are things about being able to do what you want when you want – things that are difficult to give up – even though you'll actually be miserable doing it. Miserable or not, you're still in control . . . . I imagine loss of control as not being able to be on your own if you want to. And yet, there I've been, so totally freaked out because there's not somebody there when I want them to be.

'Since starting with Mike I've felt so peculiar, like I never expected. I really didn't know that I would feel all right. It's so intense. What's struck me is that the relationships I could keep at arm's length, that didn't intrude on my being on my own, that they didn't matter. It made me look at the basis of me being on my own, what it was I was so scared of. And just knowing that somehow, if I wanted to move forward, I'd actually physically take my rules about never wanting to live with anybody, I'd actually have to face them and work through a set of things about how you managed to have a fairly close relationship. Either you have two separate places or you live together, and if you live together, certain problems follow, and if you don't live together certain problems follow.

'As for having a child, I don't want to be in a family. It fills me with complete horror, and yet I don't want to have a child alone. If living with a man is so terrifying for your own space, living with a child is a hundred times worse.

'The most difficult thing is that it's taken so long for me to discover that I can do some things by myself. If it's taken this long – and that sense is very fragile; it comes and goes – how can I even possibly sustain it with anybody else? You know, how can I keep on having some sense of myself?

'In my relationships with men it's always struck me that I've made men into fathers, then mothers. Being in a relationship allows certain things to be explored. I just feel so overwhelmed by so many things. I find it difficult to face them all at once.'

'In my relationships with men . . . I've made men into fathers, then mothers.'

Does Jenny's perception bear out Freud's observation that 'many women who have chosen their husband on the model of their father, or have put him in their father's place, never-theless repeat towards him, in their married life, their bad relations with their mother'.[1] Freud explained this as regression to the original, exclusive attachment to the mother, the first love-object, a relationship on which subsequent attachment to the father was built.

Is this a general pattern in women's relationships with men? Do we unconsciously look for daddy in men we get involved with? Could it be otherwise, when the social expec-tation of the husband/lover corresponds to that of the protector and provider? The traditional marriage ceremony begins with the bride being 'given away' by her father to a man who will replace him; this is more than outworn symbolism, even though in western marriage women give themselves freely to a husband. The man's status as head of a marriage or a household is publicly validated and economically confirmed. Men earn more than women and hold most positions of power. It is a man's world. By accepting male authority, women have a place in it and a guarantee of safety and security. This is the social bargain; the social reality is drastically at odds with it. As we get closer to this picture of the happy family contract, its contrasting background detail is revealed: the impermanence of marriage, single-parent families, the impossibility of living on a single wage (particularly for working-class women).

It's a poor bargain, but the alternatives, for most women, are not that attractive. And however much we reject it consciously as a fraud, however much we're empowered to do so by reason of our financial independence: bank account and mortgage, and a job – a place out in the man's world – that old promise of a man to take care of you will whisper from the past.

Fathers . . . will solve things, will assume the burden of hard dealings with the world, take the strain. They will impose discipline and order where women live chaos. The world is governed by the law of fathers, a law that, according to Freud, is always external for women, never internalised in the psyche, as it was for the infant boy when faced with the need to identify with the father's power through his fear of it, a fear provoked by the boy's jealous rivalry with his father for the mother.

Mothers . . . will nurture, will give us unconditional love. In our relationships with men the initial idealised image of the father may then become that of the mother – the mother who perhaps never gave us all the love and nurturance we wanted – but the two images will coexist and coincide, clash and become confused. In a partner we may seek both sets of attributes, both kinds of love; in infancy we had one love-object, the mother, on whom we were dependent until the discovery of sexual difference meant her replacement as love-object by the father.

Perhaps this duality of attachment, this desire to find both mother and father in the adult object of our love, is what sometimes makes it so difficult for grown women to 'leave home'. As Ruth Bailey has described, 'I just went from home to college to getting engaged and married; from the arms of one family into another.' She recalls, 'I don't think I was particularly a parent figure in those relationships. Somehow it was my fault if the relationship wasn't working very well. I'd just get very confused and I'd feel like a bad child with daddy.'

The parent that a man seeks in his relationships with women is the mother – only the mother, because she was his first and only love-object. The father, the male authority figure, has been integrated into his own psychic identity, perhaps only partially, but he is there, inside, allowing a part of him to be separate.

Jenny Wilmott's fear of becoming absorbed in a relationship with Mike is well grounded. She has 'left home', and created an independent life for herself without a man around; with a close involvement that echoes the symbiotic dependency of childhood she anticipates the loss of that separate adult identity.

What we unconsciously seek and what we find in our relationships are, of course, different things. But alongside the realities of what adults give and take in their emotional lives, the childhood desires reverberate and are re-enacted in fantasy and in hidden patterns of dependency. As women we have to reckon with our wish to merge with the mother *and* be protected by the father. Freud's theory of psychic development offers some clues to what underlies women's ambivalence towards independence, towards leaving home. But the insights of psychoanalysis can also help us find encouragement in our conflicts. Julie Menéndez's story illuminates some of the difficulties and at the same time the strengths to be gained in making the break from dependency.

J

ULIE MENÉNDEZ Julie Menéndez is 43. She grew up in the mid-west of the United States. In 1970 she came to London where she now paints and works as a fabric designer. She lives alone.

'What I experienced between 1965 and 1975 was a ten-year period of living with first my husband and then with another man I had a relationship with – with no break between. For that whole period I was cohabiting, at a period of my life where I should have gone for my own work. But I found I was totally frustrated, I couldn't do it. Both men were very creative, extremely creative. My husband was an actor, a successful actor, and I found at first it was a relief for me to have somebody next to me who was doing all this, therefore I was led to believe that working for him, with him was in fact being productive myself. It was giving me access to something. But in fact it wasn't, it was all his own sphere of work. But I had the illusion that I was partaking in it.

'And then I got completely overwhelmed by it, and I was very very unhappy, and instead of having the courage of going for my own initiative and actually finding things to do for myself I then found another escape through somebody else, and changed country. So the illusion was there still; I was in his context, I was mixing with his friends, I was with somebody who was recognised, who was known, who was doing tons of things – and I wasn't.

'It wasn't that I thought I wasn't good enough to do things myself. Always at the back of my mind there were things I had to do, things I wanted to do, and on the one hand I was capable of doing it, and on the other hand a huge part of me was saying no to this kind of pressure. What happened was that gradually I started hating men for doing what I was supposed to do. They were doing it; I wasn't. And in both cases it took it into the relationships; this was why the relationships ended, because of on the one hand me using them for something they couldn't possibly fulfil, while they couldn't provide me with anything at all. So it was the big daddy thing, of expecting daddy to say, 'this is it, go off little girl and do it.' Of course they were grown up men, they were independent men and they weren't going to show me how. Not at all.

'It would have been worse I suppose if one of them had done exactly what I wanted.

'So it took something absolutely disastrous for me to make the kind of decisions that are about living or dying . . . what happened was that I got pregnant in 1973 by the man I wanted to be pregnant with. But I got pregnant by mistake, and I knew very well that if I had a child then, even though part of me wanted it very badly, I knew I couldn't possibly do it, because that would be the end of my working life. And I hadn't even started, I didn't know what I wanted to do, and I knew that infant would take it over – it would have done.

'I kind of knew what it was I wanted. I'd had a fine arts training, I know it was something to do with the arts that I wanted, I knew that I wanted to go back to painting. I knew that I could do something in that area. But since I hadn't started yet on a career, I knew that giving birth would take me over completely. I couldn't then start something which I'd been delaying for the past ten years. It was one thing or the other. I was 32. I had to make up for the last ten years when I'd been doing nothing. Yet there had always been this illusion that I had been something. Because I was in a different area from the men I was with I had this identity. I was always introduced as the artist wife or whatever. But it was a complete con, because nobody had seen my work.

'First of all, it has to do with the direction I knew I wanted to take at a very early age. When I was tiny I used to draw and I thought some day I would be an artist, whatever that meant, and so I grew up with this idea, and it was very, very fixed in my mind. It was recognised in my family that I could do it, it was always taken for granted, and when I left high school and I wanted to do fine arts right away – my mother I wasn't tied to at all, and she said it's what you must do, a career and all that. So I did that. They paid for me to do it.

'I got married quickly, very young, because my background was very bourgeois, Catholic, and my husband was the one person I knew who was going against this social background, and the class thing. We were very close friends, then we decided to live together and get married. So we left together. But then he took over, he became the important one. If I'd had the guts I could have done it on my own, I could have stayed and had a flat of my own; it was my dream. But I didn't. I could only do it on the strength of somebody else. That was the 1960s.

'I was dependent on him. I *thought* I was dependent on him financially, but in fact I supported him throughout the five or six years that we lived together. I was a waitress. I didn't see it as supporting him because I was supporting him in a way that permanently I wouldn't have wanted to support myself – with very menial jobs. I took anything that came, and we used to move from one city to another all the time, because he was going from one run to the next. But he depended on me for money when he wasn't working, and my work was piecework and it was whatever paid the rent. So in fact I could have supported myself doing the same thing, but I didn't want to support myself that way. So there was a big split between the way that I was making my money then, and the way that I saw myself making money eventually. He would also say, "This is my year, and next year it's going to be for you." And one day there was success, he made money, there were television shows and so on. We were in Chicago.

'So this is what happened. We had a friend who was a film animator and I saw the films that his students were making and I thought this is fantastic, and so I started to think about that. And it was a good time for us, my husband was doing well, and the coming Christmas he gave me a rostrum camera. It was very basic, but it worked, and he built a table. And he said I didn't need to be working, I could do films. So I quit my job. And suddenly I had to produce films. So I sat at my machine for days on end; the films were there in the fridge, but I didn't know what to do. I didn't have one single idea. It was terrible. I sat there, I'd get up in the morning and I'd sit. And I didn't know what to say, I didn't know what to do. And I did that for about two weeks. And then one night a friend called me up and offered me a job for three weeks. She persuaded me, even though I was meant to be working on my films. I said I can't, because this is the beginning of my working life as an artist, but she persuaded me, just for three weeks. I felt guilty, stupid, totally inadequate, and totally empty – I couldn't even draw – so I said OK, I'll do it.

'And Joe was furious – and he was absolutely right to be. He said, "If you can't face this thing you'll never do it. You should stay there and do something . . . ." And finally I convinced him the money would help, but he was very angry. So, relieved as anything, I went down there to the club and started working, and twenty-four hours later I'd met this man, and that was it. That was the man that I finally left Joe for. It was a total escape. It all happened in a period of ten days. And then he left, and suddenly I was in love, I was desperately in love. And then it was great, I was in love, so I didn't have to worry, because it took up my time completely. I used to walk the streets of Chicago in a pink cloud, I used to spend my days waiting to get my letters. I didn't need any more justification; that filled me up completely.

'And then, after the period of being totally euphoric,

then I had to take steps, I had to come to England to
see this man, I had to consummate the affair – which
hadn't even been started yet, it was all by letter, it was
all dreams and fantasies; it was nothing physical, really
it was totally romantic. And so then there was my first
trip to England. And I came to England at least two or
three times until finally I moved here, to London. And
I'll never forget the period before. I couldn't decide to
leave Chicago. It wasn't that I didn't want to leave Joe,
so much as knowing very well that I was coming to
London without having done something first. But I chose
not to think about it. Though I started thinking about
what kind of work I wanted to be doing. It was
incredibly vague, but enough for me to think, "That's it,
when I get to London I'll do it." And I came to London.
And then I got very ill, a total depression, because it had
all been very romantic, and then I saw myself falling into
the same trap here.

'I came here in 1970. Then I was ill, then the depression,
because M was getting on with his life, and I didn't
know what I wanted to do. I had no idea. He supported
me. And I had a very good excuse; I didn't have a
working visa, so I wasn't legally allowed to work. And I
had a bit of money saved. But there was no way I could
delude myself any longer, and I got more depressed, and
through my depression I started attacking him. I was
expecting him to provide me with something that no way
he could give me. The relationship was getting worse
and worse. I went back to college for a year then, and I
got back to drawing and I did a film . . . . I remember
when I was a student I knew that the only way for me to
work properly would be for me to be on my own, but
I couldn't detach myself from M, so instead of plunging
completely into work, it would be completely half-
hearted. I'd go back to the flat, back to the marriage.

'I just could not detach myself. It was basically very

safe, he was protecting me from everything. But I knew
I had to.

'I didn't leave. He did. When I got the abortion it was
such a horrific thing for me to do, it was such a hard
decision to make, it was so painful a process, absolutely
unbearable, and I knew that I'd done something which
was strictly my own doing in a way, but I knew it was
the right decision to make. But I knew that I wouldn't
have had an abortion had I been independent, had I been
working, so the minute I had the abortion I knew very
well, from that moment on I'm going to start. There was
no way I could live with myself otherwise. The week
after, I went out and looked for work. And then for
months and months and months I went to see people,
and I got work rejected all the time. Nothing came out
of it, until the first job I got in a studio. And then things
started getting better for me.

'Through working in a commercial studio I found my
way through very negative things. Through doing what
I didn't like much, I decided what I did want to do. It
was advertising work and it came to a crunch when one
day there was a film being made for South Africa, and I
said I didn't want to work on it. And I got the sack.
There was one other person who did the same thing. He
got the sack too.

'Then M went through a lot of changes in his life. And
he decided to live on his own. It came as a complete
shock, it happened very, very suddenly. But he said, "Stay
in the flat, and I'll get a room somewhere else." And
then I did the best thing I could have done which was to
say I would move out. That also meant that really I'd
have to stand on my own two feet. I remember thinking
that if I stayed on in the flat, in my old world, I'd
probably carry on surviving, and not do much more. So
I left, and I took a room somewhere else. That happened
in December 1974. We spent Christmas together, and in
January I left. The first thing I did was to buy *Spare Rib*.

'In the process of wanting to start from scratch, where was I going to start? I had to start with my sex, it was as basic as that. I mean the women's movement was pretty strong – until then I didn't want to know because it was so threatening, and threatening to the couple. So although I listened to what people were saying, I never went to marches, I never read very much about it – I'd read Betty Friedan. I knew once you start on that road there's no way back. But now I had absolutely nothing to lose. So I started looking round, and I'd heard about *Spare Rib*, so I went off to buy it. And I got involved with one of the groups I read about there. And then it was easy. And very shortly after that – I was reading a lot of feminist books – through feminism I got into wider politics.

'It was the first time I'd ever lived on my own. Ever. I was terrified. But I had no choice; he left me. But there was no time to be scared, I had to make a living. In a funny kind of way I wasn't scared of living on my own, because of not ever living on my own before, it was new.

'I remember the terrible pain of being on my own, but I remember the thrill, the excitement of finally doing something I'd always wanted to do. I'd always wanted to live on my own, but I'd never done it. But it was always fantasy; I never saw myself when I was a child, in my wildest fantasies, as a housewife with children. I always saw that position as being totally boring, very, very traditional, and as a kid I was always very rebellious. That desire to get out always stayed; it was never crushed. I never did anything about it. Although to all appearances I was very rebellious, I was very good, I always stayed home.

'I remember the first night that I spent on my own, ever. And I remember lying in that bed, and it suddenly felt like being back in the convent, when I was at boarding school. I'll never forget that feeling of being in myself, alone, with the white curtains drawn. It's unbelievable when you're a child, that they can do that to you, leave you there. But it was also very exciting, because I'd made that decision and done things I daren't. But the thing about the convent was that it was always very safe for me, it was always safer than being home. It was the structure of an institution. So there was a sense of peace, but also of real panic. I also knew that when I got up in the morning, and I was working from nine to five, there was a structure there. Thank God, if that hadn't been there, I hate to think of it.

'Immediately I was making new relationships. Through all those years I didn't really make relationships with people. I was with men. There were associations with people, but not real friendships. The friends I chose were friends that had to do with what I started to get interested in. I'd go for people to support me.

'I've lived on my own for ten years now – there was a period when I shared someone's house temporarily – but it's been getting better and better, to the point where two and a half years ago I bought this flat, and then it was total bliss, and suddenly I realised that that's it, I was quite independent. I'd stopped relying on men for that kind of comfort, that kind of security . . . . I was very critical in the sense that I wasn't willing to compromise in the same way that I did before. It took quite a few years to see that and finally live it.

'For a long time I'd had this fixation about M. That we really should be together and that he'd made a big mistake. But then that wore off, but it took a long time. I yearned less and less. And then I went through therapy. For about three years I'd worked like crazy – the idea of work had a lot to do with my politics, and a lot to do with the safety. But then I felt I was totally hung up on this, and I had a lot of financial pressures. And I couldn't cope on my own. I went to see a therapist. There were fantastic things missing . . . .

'All through these years I had a fantastic pride. I think it had to do with the way I saw myself as a child. I had

this vision of me working as an artist, alone. That's a lot
to do with having had an older sister who . . . first of all
I grew up in a family of women who were all very strong
and very much in opposition to the only man in the
family, who was my father. My sister, who was very
talented and energetic, was very much a product of the
1950s, and she got married to get out, and she
immediately got pregnant, and she had three kids, and
she was suddenly stuck. She could have done anything,
and I remember how depressing it was to visit her, with
nappies hanging around. For me and my younger sisters
there was nothing romantic about that. She hated
housework and everything was always disgusting; there
was no charm to her set-up.

'This couple thing was always to do with the same man,
with M. Because of the way he was. He was always very
loving, very caring, and very kind. When I was ill he
looked after me. He wasn't oppressive as a husband. My
first husband was always very demanding.

'We got back together again, on and off, and now we're
together. But I don't *need* the relationship, I'm not
dependent on it. I want it at another level, I don't need
it for survival. I don't need it financially at all. If I choose
to be in that relationship it's for other reasons altogether.
It's to do with life with him being better than on my
own. It's really choice. Because life on my own is very,
very good. I think it's very crude to say that financial
independence inevitably leads to total emotional
independence. You can be independent and still
emotionally depend on others. And now I'm noticing, I
think he depends on me – much more than I knew.

'There's work. And there are also friendships that I've
developed over the last years and that are very fulfilling,
very satisfactory. I'm now as happy to see a friend as I
am to see a lover. The lover is not unique any more, he's
only part of the whole network.

'It's very, very scary to think of someone being there

again all the time, and it's got so I'm not sure how to
do it; obviously there's no blueprint for this, it's much
more to do with recognising what your needs are at the
time, and being absolutely clear about it. For the past few
months, because this relationship has started again, I
could see myself behaving in a way that I found
unacceptable, so I'd stop in my tracks and say, hey! For
example I found myself not committing myself to meeting
friends because I'm not quite sure what the man will do
that night, if he'd be here or not. And so I'd automatically
say no to the friend.

'But the thing to do is obviously to structure your time
very carefully.

'It seems totally "unnatural", but only in terms of the
past. In the light of my past there's no way that I'd ever
give up friends. I'd never do that, I can't afford to. I don't
know how close his friendships are, but he depends on
me as a person to be with. That's the case with men. But
it comes as a shock, because for the past ten years I
hadn't allowed those kinds of relationships to interfere
with my life.

'It's still terrifying as a prospect because I know what
happened in the past, and what happened was that I
could not work. Of course now it's different. I'd have to
create a totally new pattern; I've been very systematic,
which is fine for me. I've always been terrified of
attempting anything with anybody else, because of the
fear of being sucked in. And now the risk is very real. I
know that I need a fantastic amount of space, physical
space as well as psychological space. I say I'm clear about
it, but . . . .

'There's bound to be compromise. What's an advantage
in a way is his own experience with feminism in the last
ten years. There's no way he doesn't understand what I'm
talking about. He may refuse to, he may argue, but he
knows very well.

'How the hell do you achieve that balance, that state

of being yourself and at the same time being vulnerable if you're with somebody, that's the problem. I can't really see myself ever ever allowing myself to be vulnerable again.

'I can't remember him being dependent on me; I'm sure he was, but I can't remember that. And also he left me, so that proves he wasn't dependent on me. It's interesting that in the past ten years he's never been without a woman, and I've been without men – I've gone through long periods of having either no men or totally casual scenes. He's always been within a relationship, several, but he's never been on his own.'

There are five of us; women, all friends. It's a bitterly cold winter evening and we huddle close to the gas fire. But the chill still leaks in through the gap in the thick curtains. The weather gives an edge to our talk, about security and worries, about the people and things that make a safety net for our anxieties. About how we shore ourselves up and feel protected from the cold blast. About who and what we depend on.

We list our worries, both real and imagined, somewhere in the future: money, illness, loneliness, growing old, being able to cope without depression, insecurities about work, children.

What if I'm ill, I say. That worries me, the prospect of not being able to earn my living. I don't have a job with a guaranteed income, sick pay, that kind of thing; everything depends on my initiative, my energy. If I don't work, there's no money. Then who would look after me, who would support me? I've always been able to earn money, since I was 14, the thought of not being able to appals me.

When I was ill last year, says R, I panicked. You remember what I was like before I went into hospital. I thought it might be really serious; I wasn't sure until I had the operation. And then I thought I'd be stuck in that awful hospital, forgotten. But everybody rallied round, took me to the hospital, visited, took me home again, and flowers, and meals cooked for me when I was still convalescing. So I know I've got a pretty solid bunch of friends I can count on.

R lives alone. I don't. But still I have a vision of myself abandoned, stricken by some long-term disease. Who could be expected to devote their life to that kind of responsibility for another person? I couldn't. Too much sacrifice. Everything an equal partnership. No man has ever supported me financially. We lean on one another, back to back. I'm dredging up deep-seated fears about being alone, uncared for, never feeling safe.

Friends. We all agree they matter immeasurably. They're there no matter what. They mean we're not isolated, there's always somewhere else to go, not just home, not just being alone, couples, children. Support, conversations, eating and drinking, going out together. Without all that it would be impossible to stay on top of things.

Not just having friends, but having them round the corner, a short walk away. I can walk to L's flat in five minutes, to R's in less than ten, in the other direction. The three of us crow about how fortunate we are and we have other friends too in the neighbourhood. We wouldn't contemplate moving. What a difference it makes. With a quick phone call we make instant arrangements, dropping in for a cup of tea, a swim on the spur of the moment, a walk in the park. A plea for help sometimes – come round, I feel awful. We urge the other two to consider moving so we can all be together. What safety.

L goes even further. She's got to know her neighbours, relies on them too. I say I value some anonymity. She reminds me she's at home a lot with a young child, like some of the other women in her street. She has a highly developed sense of community, mutual help, practical support: babysitting, lifts, school jumble sales. Typical things women did to help one another out, before we started relying on feminism.

D lives alone with her 2-year old daughter. I don't know a soul round here, she says. She doesn't want to either. I've got my friends, they visit me, I visit them. But I prefer my privacy, my complete independence; I don't want the neighbours to know all about me. I don't want to be invaded.

We ponder the meaning of community, family. None of us has daily links with parents, siblings. We've all moved away from where home once was. Education, London. Women making our way in the world. Ideological rejections of the family. We know it's too enclosed, too exclusive, too oppressive. But what's replaced it? We need something: structure, ritual, pattern, somewhere we feel sure we belong.

The women's movement, or its remnants. Is that enough? No, not enough to stop loneliness. A speck in the urban dust. Chaos. But it helps: more closeness to other women, networks, advice and emergency support, feminist first aid.

D says the left has overlooked people's needs for ritual; for weddings and funerals, for ceremonies that celebrate or heal. Without them we feel adrift, not part of something that has continuity. We could have other ceremonies, though with different, better meanings. Changing the way things are.

We thought we would once. The counter-culture. Politics. Children of the 1960s and all that. Smashing oppressive institutions. Where are we now in the 1980s with middle age on the horizon? No diamonds in the sky out there. Cold air. No brave new world, but retreats, back to 'the family'. Fewer communes, more couples. Digging in.

R is alone, D is alone, H shares a house with a woman friend, and has a boyfriend who lives on the other side of London; she sees him only at weekends. I don't really feel I'm in a couple, she says, though it's been years; I cope with most things on my own.

And I don't. The couple helps. I feel defensive. I feel there's no virtue in this. I know how hard it is to cope on your own. I did it. No one there to lean on. But this isn't easy either. Compromises. Someone else's moods, problems, obsessions. No way out through them, getting sucked in. Being dependent. Juggling two sets of contradictions. L talks about it too. Another couple.

It's got colder. The winter of '85. The coffee-pot's empty. Someone closes the gap in the curtains, pulling them together. In another room the baby cries. D disappears, comes back a little while later with a bottle of wine. She pours, we all drink, warmed, luxuriating. Then it's late. We go home, our separate ways.

CHAPTER 3

LEAVING HOME

In 1966, when I was 19, I read Simone de Beauvoir's *The Second Sex*. Over the years since then I've learned that many other young women first read it around the same time; their introduction to feminist ideas, as it was for me.

No other book comes close to this one's revelatory status. It occurs repeatedly as a landmark on biographical maps of political change, as women describe how they were drawn towards the women's movement in the 1970s. It belongs to the category of 'books that changed my life'. Yet we all seemed to have read it in isolation, stumbling across it without any context but our separate individual histories.

Of course 'we' tended to be young educated women. I was in my third year at university when a friend, Catherine, pressed the battered, dog-eared paperback on me enthusiastically, insisting that I read it. When I did, I was quite stunned. I don't think I had ever read anything before that provoked such strong feelings: outrage at the injustice of it all, at the sense that something had been falsified in my picture of life, and, more dimly, a sense of grievance that the suddenly recognisable truth of de Beauvoir's account burdened my future.

I seethed, for a long time after reading the book, but it didn't occur to me that anything might be done to change things. Catherine, it seems in retrospect, took it more personally than I did. The book gave her ammunition for argument; she complained a lot about the way the social odds were stacked against women, argued forcefully against the idea of female inferiority, and made a strong case for herself as a would-be businesswoman and success story. She had a keen sense of her own potential and saw being a woman as a handicap to her ambitions. I couldn't think at that time what my potential might be, and what difference it would make that I was a woman. But *The Second Sex* still moved me to anger on behalf of womankind.

I read a lot, but I was no intellectual. The same went for my friends, Catholic girls, mainly from working-class backgrounds, who saw university as a means to an end. A career might be pursued (as a teacher, for most) but it was to be reconciled with marriage and children.

Our tastes and ideas were no doubt parochial compared with those of students in the more sophisticated English universities – where ideas were valued for their own sake, and where perhaps common rooms and women's halls buzzed with talk about Simone de Beauvoir. Who knows? Maybe they even did in Glasgow, somewhere. But my corner of the 1960s was a lot more homespun. I talked to no one but Catherine about this book that both of us found so disturbing. After a few months its echoes abated, and it was stored away to join the rest of the clutter in my head, perhaps gnawing at my perceptions, but in an unconscious way, only to be retrieved and understood again through the filaments of memory and through a shared new understanding about women that came a long time later.

Adrienne Rich wrote in 1971, 'in the last few years the women's movement has drawn inescapable and illuminating connections between our sexual lives and our political institutions. The sleepwalkers are coming awake, and for the first time this awakening has a collective reality; it is no longer such a lonely thing to open one's eyes.'[1]

Her metaphor serves me well. Written in 1949, *The Second Sex* seeped slowly into the consciousness of a generation coming of age in the 1960s. Its insights opened my eyes; but it was a lonely thing. Without any connection to the rest of the world, or to other bits of one's own world, what do you do with such discoveries? You go back to sleepwalking, only your dreams are now coloured by what was learned in wakefulness.

*   *   *

At 19 I had a double-sided vision of my future. After university I would travel, perhaps live abroad; with a degree I would find work easily, well-paid and interesting work (I was vague about this, but confident that 'the world was my oyster'). I was equipped by education for an independent life, for complete economic independence, which I had had partially from the age of 14, when I began doing cleaning and waitressing jobs, then shop work, in the school holidays; by the time I was 17 I had a university grant and supported myself with jobs between terms.

The other side of the future was marriage and children. It was certainly what was expected for me – but my peers, by my family, by the culture I lived in – so I expected and desired it, because it was how life was meant to be. The alternative was loneliness and failure. This was not to say that I was happy with these prospective arrangements, but the prospect was so distant and insubstantial that I was certainly not unhappy.

In the end it was only the first version of the future that came true. A number of my friends rushed to the altar immediately after graduation, or on completion of a postgraduate teacher training course, and within a year or so the first babies were announced. I half-envied them the weddings, though not the babies. Soon after, I left on my travels.

I lived abroad, then in London, went abroad again twice to live, and finally settled down in London some ten years ago. Life had been more complicated and difficult than I had imagined, although it was not without some equally unforeseen and compensatory excitements. The essential details: I did not marry, did not have children, remained financially independent. These days I share flat ownership and everyday life with the man I met five years ago.

The outlines of my individual story are characteristic of a generation of women leaving higher education and stepping into a world where, without any shadow of graduate unemployment, we could make our own futures. Of course it was a world in which a woman couldn't get a mortgage on her own, in which abortion was only just legalised (in 1967) and in which it was harder than it is now for unmarried women to obtain contraception. But it offered us, and in greater numbers than ever before, the prospect of genuine economic independence.

For many women I know with that shared history, and a number whose voices appear in these pages, the issue of economic dependence on a man has not been a pressing one, or it has been only for brief periods. Some married then entered the statistics of the rising divorce rate (in 1980 six times what it was in 1961); some didn't marry at all, embarking on couple relationships that followed the pattern of serial monogamy or cohabitation; some are lesbians; some went through the lifestyle politics of communal living and multiple relationships that flourished in the early to mid-1970s. Before the 1960s such a large-scale deviation from the conventional route map of female expectations had never happened; it was unthinkable. Surely this should give pause for thought about the links between economic and psychological independence?

Of course motherhood is the wild card, however neatly you stack the pack. But here too is a panorama of change, with the reshaping of family structures that was a consequence of divorce and separation, and of other trends (over 70 per cent of all households in Britain defy the traditional family pattern). As well as choosing not to marry, many women of my generation have *chosen* to have a child outside marriage, something that was simply economically impossible until the advent of the welfare state in the late 1940s, and continued to bear a crushing social stigma right up until the 1970s. Single motherhood – and eight out of nine single parents are mothers – is for many synonymous with hardship, but alongside the majority who live on social security benefits, there is also a small but significant minority of women who combine a job or career of some kind with single parenthood.

This proliferation of personal choices has both followed and quickened the current of social and political change. The sleepwalker can only truly wake up when there is a collective validation of perceptions and experience. At the height of its early optimism, the women's movement illuminated women's social situation with startling brilliance. The past, the present, and the way to the future were instantly made clear in a vision of simple transparency. That, at least, is how it seems, now that the fluctuations of politics and the elaborations of our knowledge have unearthed knotty complexities and made both history and our possibilities denser, more opaque.

In the face of pervasive economic and political pressures, and a climate of conservatism that gives ideological weight to the values of traditional femininity and familial roles, the women's movement in the 1980s has lost its momentum and coherence. Yet many women for whom 1970s' feminism was a central, revelatory experience recognise that that coherence could only be short-lived. The character of the women's movement, a fragile coalition of campaigns and philosophies, could under no circumstances have remained static. The divisions and splits that occurred were a part of the movement's growth, its loss of innocence.

Among women who cherished the sense of belonging that was to be found in a unified movement, this process has caused some demoralisation, threatening a return to the isolation from which they had once been rescued by the expression of female solidarity. But the fragmentation of feminism into different feminisms has also coincided with a more diffuse acceptance of its ideas and aims, and a greater confidence on the part of women in general.

It is a confidence that rests on changed common sense definitions. If the women's movement articulated collectively what women knew individually but was unspoken because there were no words for it, the last few years have shown that the words, once found, have entered the common language of everyday life, at least to the point where they are no longer strange, and often gaining a supple familiarity. The assumptions of language have been challenged, and there has been the development of a vocabulary which conceives of women in a much richer and more varied way than was possible twenty years ago.

Of all the political and social movements that grew out of the last two decades, it was the women's movement that gained the most secure cultural footing. Ten years of feminist publishing, with some half dozen feminist imprints (beginning with Virago in 1976), and a studied attention to women as a market for their books by the longer established publishers, have confirmed and reflected this. It has created a collective context for the reading and understanding of new books and reprints, and the existence of such a body of literature – fiction and non-fiction, popular and academic – also means that neither are other kinds of books read in isolation. The growth of feminist literary criticism, together with the evidence of feminist research across a range of disciplines, give us new ways of looking at what women wrote in the past; and we can bring our changing pictures of women's place in history, in social and political life, to a wide range of writers, male and female, for when we read, we enter a dialogue. The meanings and truths to be found in, say, a novel, are not fixed and timeless, but vary according to the reader's perceptions and experiences. The knowledge that our particular responses may be *shared* within a culture can also confer meaning.

What are the books now being read by young women coming to feminism for the first time, that compare with the significance of *The Second Sex* for young women in the 1960s? The question cannot be answered, the hypothesis of an analogous solitary reading experience is meaningless, precisely because of what has happened in the intervening years. Then, feminism as a movement or as a socially expressed set of ideas was still some years round a corner in the future, or was an old-fashioned word that belonged round a corner in the distant past. Now, young women bring a cultural knowledge of it with them to their reading, or soon find this confirmed elsewhere. They are living inside a visible process of change which can offer them some support and much information with which to puzzle out their own choices.

How does this awareness of cultural and social affirmation affect a sense of individual autonomy? There are still enormous influences that prevail in favour of traditional relationships between the sexes, and a world built on female inferiority and exclusion, but the ambivalence and the conflicts that are the product of these must surely be made all the more distinct. The existence of many different versions of femininity, many different female viewpoints and possibilities for women, must give psychological weight to the potential for self-definition.

The economic dimension of women's lives is crucial; even *some* degree of financial independence can make a huge difference to a woman unaccustomed to having any money of her own. Clearly, there is a relationship between women's economic status in the overall picture of society, and how the picture conveys women's strengths and potentials, although it may be a rather messy and contradictory relationship.

In the late 1970s a well-known advertisement for Virginia Slims cigarettes used to tell us that we had 'come a long way'. The jokey visual comparison was between the confidently smiling image of the liberated, unconfined modern woman, and her Victorian or Edwardian counterpart, socially restricted and physically constricted by the tightness and stiffness of contemporary fashion. The gap that now exists between the broad social validation of women's claims to a better deal and the shrinking possibilities for these to be given political and economic priority is proof enough that this glib idea of an inevitably progressive emancipation falls far short of reality.

In the 1980s, women's expectations are of a different order from what they were in the 1960s. Then, they were buoyed up by a general mood of historical optimism that took the future for granted – things would just get better and better. Now, mass unemployment and a severely battered welfare state leave no room for such illusions. But women's greater confidence has at the same time sharpened aspirations. Change is uneven and often peculiarly belated, sometimes out of step with the signs of the present, still catching up with the promises of the past.

One example of this is the Ford machinists' strike, which held enormous symbolic significance for the gathering women's movement. In 1968 women machinists sewing seat covers at the Ford motor factories in Dagenham and Halewood came out on strike. The issue was the grading of their work, which was classified as unskilled. They demanded recognition that it was on a par with the semi-skilled production work performed mainly by men. They made history as the first group of women trade unionists to go on strike for equal pay.

The dispute was settled without the women's demands being fully met, but with a compromise 95 per cent of the semi-skilled rate of pay, achieved when the Employment Secretary, Barbara Castle, entertained the women to tea, in the publicly non-confrontational industrial relations style of the day. (Barbara Castle herself had in the 1950s been an active supporter of equal pay, when the campaigns for equal pay for women teachers and civil servants were to the forefront.)

The outcome was hailed as a victory by equal pay campaigners. It's not difficult to see why. The Ford women had improved their situation, and just as women teachers and civil servants had finally reached equal pay in 1961 by a series of stages, so the expectation must have been that in this case too things could only get better.

In November 1984 women sewing machinists at Ford's Dagenham plant came out on strike with exactly the same demand for regrading. Some were veterans of the first strike. The following year, after the dispute had gone to arbitration, they finally won.

In 1984 women's basic weekly earnings were 73 per cent of men's, only a small improvement on 1975, when the Equal Pay Act was passed.

The harsh truth is that within the structures of the national economy women's status as paid workers has changed very little since the late 1940s when Clement Attlee's Labour Government of post-war reconstruction expressed a policy of welcoming large numbers of women into the labour force as a temporary measure, because they were needed in the booming new industries and the newly-founded welfare state. It was a policy that clearly defined women as a 'reserve army of labour' whose primary place was still in the home, to which they would be restored once the emergency was over. Yet according to a Government survey of women and employment published in May 1984,[2] ten million women in Britain are paid workers – 40 per cent of the labour force – and the evidence shows that women are spending an increasing proportion of their lives in employment, returning to work far sooner after childbirth than they did twenty-five years ago.

Everywhere, images and ideas about women conflict and compete, depending on their source; different bodies of knowledge have their own histories, their own framework into which male and female characteristics and relationships are obliged to fit. Since the society we live in is built on hierarchies of class, gender and ethnic division, which are reflected in economic terms, then many interests are threatened by profound disturbance of these. So public meanings are at war. The page 3 tabloid image of women objectified persists; the soap powder ads that suggest a nation of full-time housewives still punctuate television programmes; despite the Sex Discrimination Act taxation laws still classify men and women differently, with a 'married man's allowance' that assumes the husband as the breadwinner and head of household, perpetuating a view of women as secondary.

But increasingly, the television dramas and soap operas that are the backdrop to the supermum ads might offer female characters of some complexity and storylines that refer to contemporary feminine problems and predicaments. This is by no means a radical overhaul of women's images (for one thing television has yet to turn its back on crass stereotypes), but it is a sure sign of how much an insistent agenda of questions about women's choices and how these are circumscribed has moved from the margins of culture to the very centre of mass audience attention.

Among the plethora of public images and exhortations that confront young women today, women's magazines must continue to exert substantial influence. Many of these have changed in ways that echo and confirm altered definitions of women's status. The appearance of the newer glossies – *Honey, Cosmopolitan* and *Company* in the 1960s and 1970s – *Options* and *Working Woman* in the 1980s – was itself the product of changes in women's roles and how they were seen as consumers. While long-established weeklies like *Woman, Woman's Own* and *Woman's Weekly* concentrated on home and family concerns, addressing the reader as either actual or potential wife and mother (and their advertisers doing likewise), the new glossies aimed for the growing numbers of women who were either unmarried and financially independent or were combining domesticity with work outside the home – and with the kind of spending power that attracted different kinds of advertising. Their aspirations were perceived as going beyond, though not incompatible with, marriage and children.

The image of this kind of new woman is most closely identified with *Cosmopolitan*, a title imported to Britain from the United States in 1972 and at the last count published in seventeen editions across the world. Feminists over the years have variously welcomed, attacked, lamented and berated the magazine's creation of the 'Cosmo girl', the idealised independent woman, glamorous, sexually active, and in control of a career-oriented, well-heeled lifestyle. Certainly, *Cosmopolitan* offered a progressive redefinition of women as autonomous sexual beings, freely seeking pre-marital pleasure in the age of the Pill. (Indeed marriage itself ceased to become an inevitable fact of the future, with the endorsement of the live-in or live-out lover.)

This broke the traditional magazine cycle that placed women on a continuum where youthful romance gave way to domestic concerns. In *Cosmopolitan* and subsequently in other glossies, women were the *subject* rather than the confused objects of sexual desires, and their lives centred on themselves rather than on the home.

Meanwhile some of the home-centred magazines (notably *Woman and Woman's Own*) were also influenced by feminism, encouraging women to look beyond the confines of the home, sometimes dedicating their pages to campaigns for a better deal on such things as childcare provision, married women's taxation and social security benefits – supporting a view of women's right to a social identity that is not just that of the housewife and mother, and recognising that it is women who bear the heaviest burdens of inequality. *Woman's Own* in particular was known for its campaigning efforts in the 1970s.

Between 1960 and 1980 the women's magazine audience became more up-market, at the same time as it became younger, with the advent of the new glossies; young women with spending power increasingly entered the scene and the freewheeling single was firmly established as a consumer. But even while they advocate progressive new versions of femininity these magazines send out contradictory messages. Ads are often in flagrant opposition to editorial statements. And the messages have been subtly altered from year to year as falling circulations in the 1980s have dictated a search for novel formulae and new target audiences. As the 1980s drew in, the impact of feminism became blunted, and home concerns (knitting patterns and recipes, advertisements for kitchen products) surfaced for the first time in *Company* and *Cosmopolitan*; and the focus on serious issues like rights at work, unemployment, politics and anti-nuclear protest had to be softened by fluffier features that emphasised 'fun' and 'femininity'.

But what has been consistent, whether the content has been radical or traditional, has been the tone. It is a tone that assumes the need to instruct the reader or chivvy her along, though sufficiently personalised and intimate to avoid any hint of talking down to her, suggesting instead a world of clubby togetherness. For young women it is the voice of the older sister who is just one or two jumps ahead in worldly wisdom and in her knowledge of the latest trend. Perhaps this is evident only in a headline or in the introductory paragraph to an article, or it may colour an entire piece of writing, but the magazines are packed with advice, with 'how-to' and encouraging imperatives.

The belief that the reader needs guidance for self-improvement, whether cautionary or permissive, is rampant, and explicit in the ethos of most of the magazines, from the glossy monthlies to the homely weeklies. I remember an editor once receiving a proposal I put to her for an article with the observation that it was 'very interesting, but how would it *help* our readers?'; I know one freelance writer who was asked to re-shape a personal account of her experiences in a way that would be more instructive to readers: 'tell them what they can learn from what you've been through.' There is no room (other than in perhaps the fiction department?) for the reader to make her own interpretations or draw her own conclusions; social or philosophical inquiry, if it exists, is at the service of psychological utilitarianism.[3]

This tutelary approach is firmly tied to historical ideas about femininity, and the importance of educating young women to the feminine role, ideas that originated specifically in the nineteenth century, as the new middle class created in the wake of industrialisation made its way in the world, confident in its ability to move upwards by virtue of industry and individual effort – an outlook summed up in the bible of the Victorian work ethic, Samuel Smiles's 'Self Help'.

The Victorians' hard-edged and ruthless doctrine of public striving in the market place had softer, humanised reflections in the middle-class home, whose duties, Christian decencies and decorum were of course women's responsibility. To know these, and to perform them with correctness and the gentility required of a middle class as yet not altogether certain of its position in society, was synonymous with 'femininity'. As Deborah Gorham observes in *The Victorian Girl and the Feminine Ideal*,[4]

> A man could achieve success through hard work and initiative, and thereby gain economic power, but his social status, if not actually determined through the family he established, was reflected through it. The style of family life, the quality of domesticity achieved, was the final determinant of the niche he occupied in the social structure.

The Victorian view of femininity was grounded in and constructed on an idea of social class and its attributes; it was an attribute of proper middle classness. Femininity was something to be learned, to be achieved through self-improvement with an exemplary goal in mind. The model, an idealised image of sheltered, delicate girlhood – the 'angel in the house' – dependent and submissive and only studious in as much as her intellectual capacities might make her a suitable companion and listener for a future husband, was one that many middle-class girls could not uphold, since financial circumstances often obliged them to find ways of earning a living. But the conception of its limits centrally shaped their lives.

Feminine limits and precepts were outlined in the women's magazines and advice manuals that proliferated from the mid-nineteenth century onwards. The first mass circulation magazines aimed at women, and quite different in character from the small number of eighteenth-century periodicals read by upper-class 'ladies' (which were often as concerned with political ideas and news from abroad as they were with fashion and home management), these are in a direct line with the women's magazines of today. Even though their content may seem light years away from the modern messages of the glossies on today's news-stands, and the lofty superiority of tone with which their counsels were delivered has been replaced by the blandishments of another age, there is a fine underlying strand of continuity. You have to learn how to be the kind of woman who is happy, successful and fulfilled in today's world; to do this you are in need of advice, you must follow an example, you must improve yourself.

The necessity of self-improvement, with its attendant denial of women's right to judge for themselves and to believe in themselves, is more than just a whispered echo from the Victorian past. It has run through educational theory and its practice in the classroom well into the second half of this century; it imbues many contemporary institutional attitudes to women (the medical establishment and the prison system stand out as classic examples of how women are infantilised in relation to structures of knowledge and power); and because of its historical tenacity, it casts a shadow of a doubt on the self-perceptions of women who nowadays expect to think and judge for themselves. Self-doubt, and a nagging awareness of our imperfections, help maintain the gap between potential and fulfilment of it. Women have to struggle against a deep-rooted lack of self-confidence that derives from a socially constructed view of femininity.

This discrepancy between, on the one hand, women's enhanced expectations of equality, their perceptions of their rights and what should be their status in the world and, on the other, the vulnerability of their own self-image was obliquely reflected in a report published by the Department of Education and Science in 1983, the most comprehensive survey of its kind ever carried out, looking at young people's experiences, attitudes and expectations.[5]

Overall, the evidence indicated a far greater degree of conservatism on most questions than might have been expected from 14–19-year-old respondents. The striking exception was in the section of the survey headed 'Feminism'. Here the majority of both sexes dissociated themselves from traditional views of women's roles, though statistically the girls were far ahead of the boys in their vision of fair shares.

- 88% of the girls thought that *employment is equally important to both sexes.*
- 80% of the girls believed in *equal pay for both sexes.*
- 93% of the girls thought that *working couples should share housework* – and 86% thought that men should be equally expert at shopping and housework.
- A mere 10% agreed with the statement that *a woman's place is in the home.*

At odds with these convictions of the need for sexual parity were the girls' perceptions of themselves and their implicit potential to achieve it. They described themselves as more nurturing and less outwardly directed than the boys. They totalled much higher percentages when applying the following descriptions to themselves: helpful, loving, reliable, obedient, nervous, worried, shy, sometimes lonely.

At the same time the boys rated themselves much more highly in terms of confidence and self-esteem – 43 per cent of the boys saw themselves as 'good-looking', and only 29 per cent of the girls; 38 per cent of the boys judged themselves 'clever', and only 26 per cent of the girls.

These are telling statistics, for they encapsulate not only the descriptive detail of stereotypes, but also their internalised realities. Insofar as girls *are* less confident than boys, more fearful and socially withdrawn, it is a measure of how profoundly enduring are cultural notions of what is 'feminine'. The feelings of inadequacy that lie behind such low self-ratings are tragic testimony to the patterns laid for adulthood.

The mismatch is familiar – between the affirmation, in the abstract, of women's equality and freedom from traditional roles of subordination to men, and the deeply lodged doubts about personal strengths and abilities. Our aspirations, and those of young women today, are stretched much further than what earlier generations could hope for; but they collide continually with the shapes the world imposes on our images of ourselves.

In a survey of 200 young women aged 16 to 20, published in the *Sunday Times Magazine* in August 1985, the respondents echoed the aspirations to sexual parity recorded in the DES report. Most expected to settle down with a partner and have children, but nearly 70 per cent wanted to get their own lives under way first. The same proportion said they would expect a partner to share housework and childcare equally, and 68.4 per cent thought they would be happy reversing traditional roles, earning the money while their partner stayed at home to look after the children.

When I talked to two groups of young women at an inner London summer school in 1983, a similar outline of expectations emerged. All were sixth formers (though from different schools), with an average age of 17. Out of twenty-one, three had strong feelings about not wanting to marry; the others felt they probably would, and although the option of 'living together' didn't seem viable at this point in their anticipated future ('your family expects you to get married'), it was something several thought would become more acceptable later on. Late twenties was generally agreed to be a reasonable age for settling down – except in the case of the Asian girls, who explained that they would be expected to marry young – '19 or so' – although attitudes to this were becoming more flexible as more of them went on to higher education.

All of these young women were preparing for A-levels, and the majority hoped to go on to degree courses or further education of some kind. This means they were neither typical nor representative of young women at large. For me, however, they offered points of comparison with my younger self, some twenty years before.

We gather in a circle, noisily, the tubular-framed chairs scraping the floor as they're pulled into place out of their classroom rows. Some girls are still in school uniform, some in colourful summer cottons, and Pratibha in the Muslim girls' baggy trousers and tunic. They're a multicultural bunch: Afro-Caribbean, Indian, Pakistani, Greek Cypriot, mixed with the paler Anglo-Saxons. I tell them I'm writing a book about what independence means to women in their everyday lives, and want to ask them some questions. In the end, the questions trigger discussions and disagreements. Two of the girls, too shy to talk, are silent, but listen.

The following extract suggests some of the ambivalence, as well as the confidence, that enters young women's view of the future.

Children

ANDREA: 'I don't want to be a mother *young*. I think you've got to be completely settled and secure in yourself and your job and who you're living with or married to, before you even contemplate having children. I would think that to get married really young after you've had an education is a waste . . . . I would think that all of us here expect to do some decent work before we settle down.'

QUESTION: 'Would better childcare facilities and other factors influence your decision to have children younger?'

ANDREA: 'I want the experience of what it's like to have children. What's the point of going through having children and then not having the experience? At least you or your husband should have it, or both.'

HELEN: 'A mother gives up her life entirely for her children.'

ANDREA: 'Well, I think maybe when they're very young.'

HELEN: 'I don't think they care who's looking after them.'

PAT: 'My brother and his girlfriend ask me to babysit. They're not married, they've got a child. The child can be just as happy with me. But I mean the mother should still think that she's got responsibility for the child.'

ANDREA asks why it should be the mother who loses her job

when children have to be looked after, and describes one
of her teachers, married to a barrister, who is swopping
roles and going on with her job while her husband looks
after the baby.

HELEN: 'There's social pressure on the woman to be a good
mother. Even if you go to the pub and leave the baby
for an hour with a baby sitter, you're neglecting it.
Women give up their lives completely when they have
babies.'

QUESTION: 'Could that be different.'

ANDREA: 'I think you've got to get a fairly good balance.
I don't think it's good to be with a baby all the time and
give up everything for it. My mum was saying the other
day what happens if you have a child on your own. She
said it's lonely, you don't get any independence, you feel
tired and you haven't got anyone to share the child with.
The child's with you all the time and you're with the child
all the time. You've not got anyone to say I'll make you
a cup of tea, sit down and I'll do it.'

SHARON: 'But now there's such a choice. You can choose
to have children or not. I know accidents do happen and
people get pregnant, but you have got the opportunity of
terminating that pregnancy.'

NASSIM: 'It's extremely difficult now. Two doctors have to
give their approval.'

I asked if anyone actually believed abortion is wrong.
There's general agreement that it shouldn't be used as a
form of contraception, and with this view: 'It's slightly
wrong, but you've got to accept that. It isn't very nice.
In certain cases it's necessary, but it would be better if
there was more freely available contraception.'

HELEN: 'Now they're making abortion harder, to keep
women at home, so that women will look after children
and not go on the dole.'

Parents

QUESTION: 'Do you think girls have more trouble detaching themselves from the family than boys?'

ALL: 'Yes.'

ELENA: 'My dad says to my brother, "How did you get on last night," you know, with a girl. And with me it's what's that love bite doing on my neck. It really gets up my nose, because he's only a year older than me, and it's such a difference between a boy and a girl.'

ALL: 'It's true.'

PAT: 'My brother can do what he wants, come in when he wants, he could stay out all night and it would still be all right, though she'd worry about him. But she wouldn't stop him from doing anything. Even if I come back late and she's not going to tell me what time to be in, she'll still expect to see me.'

QUESTION: 'What reasons do parents give for this double standard?'

CLAUDIA: 'Mine think of me as a flower; you know, a *flower*, and if you get pregnant you'll die' (general laughter).

ELENA: 'My parents are really strict when it comes to me going out. They tell me what time to be in, and if I want to stay out I'll stay out. But my brother phones up and says he's going to stay out a couple of days – he's 19 .... When it comes to my dad being worried about me getting pregnant him and my mum argue about it. My dad says he's not worried about my brother, but my mum says, "If he gets somebody pregnant it's someone else's daughter," and he says, "So, she's had it." '

Mothers

SHARON: 'I feel totally that I'm responsible for my mum, and anything that I do I think what she . . . .'

PAT: 'I always worry about my mum.'

ANDREA: 'They get worried about you and you feel guilty.'

HELEN: 'She's always worrying about me and . . . I don't want to end up like her!'

ANDREA: 'I don't know what they think. They must think we've never heard of contraception. They must think we go out and do it all the time' (laughter).

SHARON: 'I feel really pleased because I'm trusted. She really trusts me. She lets me go on holiday, on the premise that we'd have single rooms. She really does trust me. I feel really responsible for my mum.'

HELEN: 'I think that's really bad though. It can muck up your brain.'

SHARON: 'I mean my mum hasn't got anyone else. I'm really afraid to upset my mum because she just hasn't got anyone – other than me and my sisters and brother. I'm more responsible for my mother than the rest of my family – I'm the only one at home.'

PAT: 'I feel like that as well. Are you afraid about getting married and that?'

SHARON: 'Yes.'

PAT: 'I think about that all the time.'

ANDREA: 'Me and my mother don't get on very well. I don't know what's going to happen if I'm the only one that sees her and all that. She's got no one else and she hasn't got a lot of friends or anything.'

HELEN: 'If they had a 24-hour childcare shop kids wouldn't be so dependent on their parents. I think it really is bad because it messes up your life.'

SHARON: 'Some parents only have kids to relate to. My mum – she's got no friends; she's got family.'

HELEN: 'She probably gave up a lot of her friends and independence when she had children.'

SHARON: 'I think a lot of people have children for company.'

QUESTION: 'How do you think you've learned from the experience of your relationships with your mothers? How do you think you'll be different with your own kids if you have any?'

PAT: 'I know my mum depends on me. My brother – she knows that he's more outgoing than me, but anything that she's not sure about, she'll ask me if I'll go with her. And I'll say yes, because I know she wants me there. And I know all her little secrets. I won't make her feel bad, I know she's done enough for me when I was young. And it's some kind of repayment. Not just trying to help her out.'

HELEN: 'My mum done that once. She came in a little bit drunk. She went to a party at my dad's work. And she came back and she started telling me her problems. And I thought, look I don't want to know, because I don't want to get twisted up. And I think that's what happens.' (The others react with visible embarrassment to what Helen has said.)

ANDREA: 'But I think it gives you a sort of insight into what's going on in your life too. And when you get to their age you're not so sure . . . .'

HELEN: 'But that's what's wrong with you. You'll get so twisted up over other people's problems you can't cope with your own.' (The others disagree with this.)

LEONORE: 'When my mum was in hospital I had to go and see her. My brother he can't stand down hospital, right, and *I'm* to be the one who has to go and see my mum. And I thought, if I don't go and see my mum who's going to go and see her. She won't have nobody.'

ANDREA: 'I was getting all the family problems – like my mum and dad had me, got married, got divorced within two years, and I was getting all the aggro from that.'

HELEN: 'I just keep away from those problems as much as I can. I love my mum, but I don't want to know her problems.'

LEONORE: 'Your mum's a part of you though, I mean.'

PAT TO HELEN: 'But say you had a problem, and you went to your mum and your mum said to you, I don't want to know. How'd you feel?'

HELEN: 'I wouldn't go to her. My mum gets jittery anyway,

I wouldn't go near her . . . . I was close, that's why I
think I'm trying to get away. Because I don't think it's
good. I think it's really horrible. I had an argument with
my mum once, and I hated her, I really did. And she said
to me, anyway parents are expected to love their kids
too much. And afterwards she told me she meant nothing
by it. But I thought God you don't love me, and I love
you completely, absolutely completely. And I couldn't
believe it.'

ANDREA: 'That's a good point. Children love their parents
absolutely.'

Friends

HELEN: 'I have a very good friend. I can tell her absolutely
anything. I mean she's mainly taken over from my mum.
I don't bother my mum. I know my friend wouldn't let
me down ever.'

SHARON: 'I've never had a best friend who was *the* friend.'

ANDREA: 'When I have best friends I don't necessarily go
out with them all the time. But it's just the sort of person
where you've got a very close relationship. I think it's
that, I don't think it's the person that you solely rely on.
It's like having a sister really.'

QUESTION: 'Girls feel less free to do certain things on their
own than boys, don't they?'

ALL: 'Yes.'

SHARON: 'You won't go to the club on your own.'
Several point out that you can be left in the lurch by a
friend if she finds a boyfriend.

HELEN: 'I hate girls who give up everything totally for a
bloke.'

ELENA: 'Give up what?'

HELEN AND OTHERS: 'All their friends.'

HELEN: 'And talking about it continuously. You know I've
got a friend, her boyfriend packed her up about two
months ago, and she came round, and that's all I heard.

She wanted to see him. It was bugging me so much. Like *she* didn't exist, it was only him.'

SHARON: 'I think boys get sort of dependent on their mates as well. Because my boyfriend since he'd left school he'd been with his mates all the time, and they've all got girls now. Since I've been going out with my boyfriend he still keeps nights to go out with his mates, and I keep nights to go out with my mates.'

ELENA: 'I don't think you should give up your friends altogether.'

Ideal women

QUESTION: 'Are there any women in public life, in music or sport or any other area that you think of as ideal images?'

SHARON: 'I'd say my mum.'

PAT: 'I'd say *my* mum.'

NASSIM: 'My mum said to me, "The only reason I'm educating you now is that you'll be able to have a good career so that if your husband decides to divorce you you'll have something else" ' (surprised laughter from the others). 'She's not really a strict Muslim mum, I mean she's quite liberal.'

QUESTION: 'When I was at school there were a lot of parental attitudes that it wasn't worth girls having an education, because they were going to get married.'

PAT: 'Well they still think like that.'

HELEN: 'Yeah. If my mum sees an old lady that's not married, well obviously nobody asked her. My brother always takes the piss – oh, she's not a real woman because she's not married and hasn't got ten kids around. They have this idea that you're not a real woman.'

SHARON: 'My sister's really independent. She has a lot more money than her husband, she's a social worker and she works late all the time, and my family sort of joke about it – oh poor old Brian. And his family are really old-fashioned; they expected my sister would be at home all the time. They knew that because she went to university obviously she would have a career, but they expected her to be home to cook his tea, because she was a woman. But I mean, Brian is great, he really is. Angela doesn't have time for housework or anything like that; she pays my mum to do her housework. I suppose if there was anybody I had to admire it would be her, because she's got such strength of character.'

HELEN: 'Does she enjoy it?'

SHARON: 'I think she puts work before Brian. She just loves her work. Their situation is a complete role reversal. But she's a person I admire, because she's always wanted to do it and she's got what she wants, and she's found someone to accept that it doesn't necessarily have to be the woman who cooks the tea. She says she would never have children. She feels that would just be too much of a tie.'

Marriage

QUESTION: 'Do you think that getting married inevitably involves giving up something?'

ALL: 'Yes'.

CLAUDIA: 'In most cases it does.'

HELEN: 'You have to give up your friends in a certain way. You can't see them as much as before. And work, with some men . . . .'

SHARON: 'When you get married I think you should discuss all these things.'

PAT: 'Say you decide you don't want children, and then someone changes their mind?'

SHARON: 'Then a sacrifice has got to be made. Either they sacrifice the marriage or she sacrifices her job.'

HELEN: 'Or they could go back to before. She could leave him so it's just like they hadn't got married anyway.'

QUESTION: 'What expectations do you have of marriage?'

ELENA: 'Well, it's one person you've got to spend your whole life with.'

HELEN: 'A lot of people don't actually spend their life with the person they marry. I wouldn't mind getting divorced. Lots of people get divorced.'

PAT: 'Why should you have to get divorced anyway? Why should you have to go into a marriage in the first place?'

NASSIM: 'I think it's easier for you lot to get divorced than for me.'

QUESTION: 'How does that make you feel about the prospect of getting married?'

NASSIM: 'Well I know I will have to get married. My mum already said, well, you know, by the age of 24. In a way I've accepted that, yes, I will have to get married some day, but to whom is up to me really. In Muslim law the girl has the final yes.'

QUESTION: 'Do you think that you have more freedom than the average Muslim girl?'

NASSIM: 'Yes.'

QUESTION: 'But you still have to get married even if you don't want to?'

NASSIM: 'Well, I had my first marriage proposal when I was 15. The boy probably saw me, but I didn't know who the hell this boy was, and I said to my mum, "Tell him to get knotted." '

Leaving home

PAT: 'I couldn't leave my mum.'

SHARON: 'I couldn't live on my own. I'd feel upset about leaving my mum. I could see myself living with a boyfriend, but I couldn't live on my own.'

QUESTION: 'What about living with other girls?'

SHARON: 'Yes. That's why it would be really nice to go to university. But deep down I don't want to go because I don't want to leave my mum. I don't know whether it's that I feel responsible for my mum or I'm dependent on my mum, or what it is; whether I feel so stuck to her that I can't, or whether my mum wants me to be there. I feel that the whole responsibility of looking after my mum rests with me. I'm the youngest. I know that she kind of agrees with that in a way, because she was the youngest in her family, and when her dad died her mum came to live with her, and *her* mum was always *her* responsibility, and she didn't shy away from that. She wanted to look after her.'

'I don't know whether it's that I feel responsible for my mum or I'm dependent on my mum, or what it is; whether I feel so stuck to her that I can't, or whether my mum wants me to be there.' In Sharon's statement of confusion about her mother there is closeness, identification, and obligation. Between mother and daughter there is a blurring of the self in duty. In herself a daughter sees what she owes to her mother, and what her mother wants from her – and finds it hard to distinguish this from what she *wants* from her mother, in what she *is* of her mother, and what she must become in her mother's image.

Much has been written about mothers and daughters; and in the last few years the mother-daughter relationship has appeared as a central preoccupation in much women's writing. How we are mothered has been seen as a vital key to the psychology of femininity, to our sense of identity and self-esteem. This has helped us to understand a lot about ourselves.

In adolescence and early adulthood, feelings around this relationship are particularly intense. To become grown up we must put a space between ourselves and our mothers, while we are at the same time ineluctably drawn back by the desire for closeness, for symbiosis. Whether that symbiosis has the lineaments of perfections or is quite frustrated hardly seems to matter; what does is the desire to sustain it or achieve it. And the desire has the double poignancy of a search in the mirror, where we may wish to see quite a different face; in our mothers we are compelled to see ourselves, in ourselves we are compelled to see our mothers. This is not meant quite literally, for with all that has been written about the mother-daughter relationship in general terms, and with however much delicacy, there is a risk of overlooking its specific quality and character. But the common coordinates of our experience are difficult to ignore, precisely because they are fixed securely by the structures of family life that are so deeply a feature of our social reality.

Women are encircled by the family. From inside that circle a young woman can see the possibilities of the world, and the need to break through the circle in order to reach them: the possibilities of being an independent adult, leaving home, getting a job, going to college, following a career, and somewhere farther out in the distance, the possibility of marriage – perhaps an equal partnership, a modern marriage, like those she sometimes sees around her.

This is one version of the passage to adulthood. In this version she will learn to take care of herself, to manage areas of her life that were hitherto in the hands of parents.

But from inside that circle a young woman has also learned another version of mature adulthood: to be an adult woman is to be a dutiful daughter, to accept the legacy that her mother gives. The duty is to stay within the family circle, if not literally then certainly at the level of an emotional surrender. Like her mother she must assume responsibility for others and their problems, she must burden herself with what troubles them, she must become a nurturer.

To refuse is no easy thing, for it entails in some sense a refusal of adulthood. The continuities of feminine experience decree that at some stage the daughter becomes the mother – often long before she herself has children. By rejecting what her mother transmits she cannot attain the status of mature and responsible adult that society approves.

To refuse is also to refuse her mother's needs, and for some daughters this degree of detachment is unthinkable. If loving closeness carries with it mutual dependency, where a mother confides in her daughter, leans on her for support, for company, as many do, then the daughter's burden of responsibility will have been accepted over years, and to deny her mother is the same as denying herself. Easier for this daughter to disappoint herself than to disappoint her mother.

If she accepts the confines of the family circle in this way, it means a part of her will never leave home, no matter what she does. She is still there, that part of her fixed in the attitude of duty, of responsibilities to be met; and perhaps, through guilt or resentment, paralysed by it, unable to take the independent action that is necessary for her to achieve what she wants. She is stuck, stuck to her mother, to the memory of a prolonged symbiosis. For boys, it dissolves as childhood trails away into puberty, or even earlier, and the circle is opened up for them; for girls, the circle has to be broken. Either way, there is a price to be paid. 'You'll get so twisted up over other people's problems you can't cope with your own . . . I don't want to get twisted up,' says Helen, defiantly rejecting her mother's example by rejecting her claims on her. She is the odd woman out.

In my head there's a fantasy mother, with wavy hair and a sparkling scarlet-lipstick smile, in high-heeled glamour and an apron frilled like the curtains on the kitchen window. She cooks; stews and and soups, of nourishing goodness and exquisite flavour. She bakes; puddings and cakes, confections of sweetness and whipped-high delight. She fills the house with the fragrance of food, and it's waiting for me. All for me. That's how a mother should be.

That men depend on women for emotional and domestic nurturance is a truism. It is so much a part of how the world is that its real implications for women are obscured or obliterated.

Yet women are seen as being dependent on men. Women are seen as curtailing male independence. The traditional drama (and comedy) of courtship and marriage as represented in popular forms of culture is that of the pursuit and capture of the woman then revealed as its own reversal: it is the female quarry who all along has been luring man into a trap of her making. Marriage is, as one Hollywood film of the 1940s (and the hit record that went with it) announced, *The Tender Trap*. And the trap is made so comfortable, so inviting and so delightful that he will have no desire to escape. When the comforts are withdrawn or refused, or when the trap becomes too restrictive, then the male impulse towards freedom asserts itself, the freedom to find another woman who will fulfil the bargain to the man's satisfaction.

Women's economic dependence on men (by the classical matrimonial arrangement) has been a perennial smokescreen for male dependence. It confirms the view of women as weak and men as strong; women as needy and men as providers, fulfilling their needs; women as inward-directed and home-bound, men as outward-directed and at home in the world. It hides the solid bedrock of female emotional strength shoring up the male edifice of self-sufficiency (while neglecting her own). Woman is the anchor without which the male pirate galleon/pleasure yacht/merchant vessel would founder. She is the safety net without which the male aerialist would never dare risk the high wire or the flying trapeze.

Cultural history weighs on us like a stone. The image of the stay-at-home is deeply embedded in its traditions. Penelope waited twenty years for Ulysses to return from the Trojan Wars, weaving her tapestry, but every night unpicking it. Sheer fidelity or a clever trick to avoid the burden of yet another husband?

Penelope after all had property and power to protect and the suitors had their eye on the empty throne as well as the empty half of her bed. Penelope's subterfuge of marital evasion belongs with those other feminine stratagems her husband has encountered in his travels: Circe's enchantment which ensnares men by turning them into Swine (here the charmer is ultimately charmed into powerlessness); the Sirens' ability to lure men to their death under the spell of their song (they are outwitted, because of Circe's advice); and the artfulness of Calypso, who is assumed to have exercised some magic on Ulysses, otherwise why would he have stayed with her for all of eight years (her gentle, loving bonds are severed only by the whim of the gods). Unlike the others, Penelope is bent on repelling male advances, but then *they* are hardly consistent in their purposes of attraction, just as likely to be mocking or malign as they are alluring. Women did not, could not wander across epic seas, so their confinement provokes quite brilliant displays of guile and deception – the frustrations of the thwarted and besieged, the ingenuity that is the response of the less powerful to their masters. Beware women, beware the tender trap; of whose making? The warning applies both ways, to both sexes; the power that women wield in the fastness of domesticity can be so easily nullified.

In Naomi Mitchison's epic fantasy of the ancient world, *The Corn King and the Spring Queen*, Erif Der, the young barbarian witch, traps the Corn King into marriage and danger at her father's behest. But change and the conflict with her husband, then with her father, send her travelling to Sparta where troubling new realities disturb the meanings of her world and its cyclical rituals, at the same time as they force her to seek new strengths in herself. Her magic and the nature of its powers alters and sometimes lessens as she encounters different forms of knowledge thrown across her path by time, place and the circumstances of her quest. What remains of her witchery is generous and benign, willed by Erif's own understandings, and it is only then that wife and husband are restored to one another.

The Spring Queen herself is trapped by the cosmos that is the source of her enchantment and can only free herself by finding or inventing other cosmologies, other possibilities within which human beings can act. To do this she has to leave behind the familiar structures and setting of her domestic power.

The domestic power that women inherit, the power bestowed on mothers and on wives, turns against them, strong though it is. It accrues at the cost of duty, sacrifice, subtle subordination. Daughters make early down payments, but history has made it a little easier for them to leave home.

CHAPTER 4

THE PRINCESS AND THE SHOWGIRL: FEMININITY AT STAKE?

When Grace Kelly married Prince Rainier in 1954, I was 7. She shimmered in my eyes. She mirrored the snowy perfection of the fairy-tale princess I had already dreamed I would myself become — either in the bliss of marriage or on discovery of my true and elevated parentage — some fine day in the future.

This is the purest and most powerful of girlish fantasies, the sublime vision of transformation in which a host of reckless imaginings are resolved. As a child I read voraciously, so much that the trance of reading was more real than anything else. So lost was I in stories that the perverse logic of fairy tales, the seemingly timeless justice of fables must have spoken to me answering both the longings of childhood and the riddles the grown-up world had set for it. Here, and in subsequent fictional worlds — where foundlings were reclaimed and rags turned to gossamer gowns, where fates were reversed in the span of a moment — I learned that it was the improbable that could be most expected. Identity (my own) had less to do with the real circumstances of my life than with something that would transcend them, just like the questing heroes and heroines in the books I read.

I had seen none of Grace Kelly's films. Nor, with the exception of Doris Day, did I make celluloid acquaintance with any of the other women stars of 1950s Hollywood who were household names: Rita Hayworth, Jayne Russell, Elizabeth Taylor, Lana Turner, Marilyn Monroe .... But the names alone had meanings, meanings soaked in scandal and glamour. Sometimes they matched a picture glimpsed in a newspaper, often they were echoed in the jokes and games shared with other children, tokens of how much you knew about the ways of the grown-up world. We skipped to play-ground rhymes with Betty Grable's legs in them.

As a Catholic child, my film-going was not only restricted to what was considered innocent and harmless, it was also governed by occasional ideas about what might positively be of moral benefit. So alongside *Snow White, Calamity Jane* and *By the Light of the Silvery Moon*, I have memories of *The Little Donkey* (a pious, sentimental and greatly enjoyable story of miraculous happenings to do with St Francis) and the more dismal *Marcelino*, which also involved a boy-hero in miracles. Being taken to the pictures was a rare treat, and film stars were generally held to be a wicked lot (except for Bing Crosby, a Catholic with umpteen children), with all that indiscriminate kissing and a divorce rate that indicated scant respect for the sanctity of marriage. There was also the 'vulgarity' of their behaviour – the physical vocabulary of sex spelled out so provocatively on the screen by the likes of Monroe and Mansfield.

The great thing about Grace was that she was a Catholic too, although until the marriage vows were made there had been no guarantee that she wouldn't 'go off the rails' like so many others the devil had ensnared as they stepped off the plane at Los Angeles airport. But the wedding to a Catholic prince and the big nuptial mass shown on television (reports were relayed from a neighbour's set) rehabilitated her completely. Rescued from the claws of sin city, her virtue now glowingly unassailable, she stood at the altar as incandescent proof that if you were to be happy, you had also to be good.

At the age I was then it was possible to ignore the additional stipulation of beauty. It was incontestable, but there was no doubt some confusion in my mind about whether beauty followed goodness or vice versa. In Grace's case the glamour was sanctified and at the same time enhanced by the combination of fairyland and Holy Mother Church. And *my* prospects were still hopeful; who could tell what I would grow up to look like?

As I grew older, the goodness issue became further compounded by looks. In the films I saw, it was always the blondes who heard the wedding bells ring for them. The brunettes, and I was one, were unlucky in love, or just plain bad. The remorseless unfairness of this made me take against the nice blondes. At school, around the age of 12, I was sorely disappointed in Ivanhoe – a fool not to fall for Rebecca. *Everyone*, including my English teacher, thought Rowena insipid.

Blondeness was femininity unadulterated. It was its own reward. Things came naturally to blondes: to their innocence and grace happiness accrued without effort. Blondes were colourless and transparent, with the blank impassivity of angels who, unlike saints, were accorded no credit for their status. Brunettes were opaque, stained with mystery, doomed therefore to inspire anxieties – towards what could not be wholly apprehended by looking – and compelled to confirm them by the necessity for action. If this feminine dichotomy was not always apparent, and was even liable to reversal, in my knowledge of books and films it nonetheless assumed the inevitability of repetition and instant recognition.

The negative (I was, alas, not blonde) gave way to the positive: repudiating the gentlemanly preference for blondes, I sought a vindication for brunettes. When, I'm not sure, but some time in my teens, on seeing Katherine Hepburn for the first time in *Stage Door* – on television. I remember being enthralled, entranced. Her accent, her upper-class origins were irrelevant, or invisible to me. I even dimly imagined that some day I might possess the same tall, long-limbed ranginess of figure, though I was short, and at 13 had once been singled out by a crassly insensitive PE teacher for being equipped with the shortest legs in the class. But the combination of characteristics embodied in Hepburn was perfect. In some essential particulars she was like me: dark, thin, bony; in others she was everything I decided I wanted to be: dazzlingly intelligent, elegant, witty, possessing a sardonic self-assurance, and never outfaced by a man.

The fact that she usually got the man – or kept him – at the end of her films was no surrender (the exception is *The Philadelphia Story*), only a vindication of all the qualities that had in the course of the narrative jeopardised her chances: her stubborness, her shrewdness, her stance of independence. When I saw *Adam's Rib* recently it came as a surprise to discover just how consciously feminist a film it was. When I first saw it, some time in the late 1950s or early 1960s it was already an 'old film' (made in 1949, the year *The Second Sex* was published) and its arguments may well have seemed like obscurely old-fashioned ones. Yet what is most vital in the film is the dramatic conflict between Hepburn and Spencer Tracy, both in the courtroom where she is defending lawyer to his prosecutor, and in their marriage, cracking under the strain of Hepburn's courtroom insistence on male-female equality. My memories of seeing her films persuade me that empathy with her screen persona and glee at the triumphs of her characters were stronger elements in my pleasure and identification than any recognition of the male-female conflicts that were being enacted. But then I hadn't lived much.

Where this leads is back to my own adolescent dilemmas over identity.

If I defined myself in relation to those iconic bearers of femininity who moved through my childhood and teenage consciousness, it was never by *simple* definition nor by passive analogy. It's true that all the potentiality of childhood – my sense of an infinite number of possible future selves – diminished as it was gradually but insistently inflected by the social divisions of gender, until the future was narrowed into an external world of adult exclusions and prohibitions. But there was that part of childhood that was chaos and curiosity, in which watchfulness and greedy attention to new things delivered unconscious, unformed knowledge as well as explained versions of reality bounded by the rules of what was then common sense. Identity: in childhood always a process of making sense, adjusting meanings, but at the same time storing away in pockets of forgetfulness those impressions and perceptions that have a different, more jagged logic – or none at all. And later the past leans on the present, the silt of memory dredged into consciousness with constant slight reminders. When the question 'who am I?' becomes 'who will I be?', the process of imaginary construction already has many elements. The little girl curled in a chair with a book, or hypnotised by the television screen, is an active participant in the fictions that absorb her.

In the muddle of fictions and fantasies that fed my childish imagination – mainly from reading, but also, as I grew older, from films and television – the sex or gender of particular characters with whom I identified mattered little. I never consciously wanted to *be* a boy rather than a girl, but at many times I must have simply forgotten that I wasn't one, so intense was my involvement in the actions and fate of male fictional characters. In inhabiting their skin there was no *gender* identification, but in vicariously living out actions that would have been outside female experience (like battle heroics or piratical adventures on the high seas) I could transcend the limits of my sex and gender in fantasy. Yet I also think I remember irritation at the absence of female characters in certain genres: in many varieties of historical adventure stories, in western films, and in Latin texts like Caesar's Gallic Wars that I studied later at school.

This kind of androgynous identification with fictional characters is of course a commonplace feature of the act of reading (whether of books or other narratives). However much intellectual distance or common sense may remind us of our position outside a story, absorption in its world means we forget we are not inside it, and this draws us into engagement with those characters whose point of view determines it, irrespective of their gender.

In childhood the aching questions of gender and identity are more easily subdued in the imagination than later, as adolescence approaches. In my own Grace Kelly phase, the acme of femininity was embodied in one shining figure after another, from the dispossessed orphan whom a magical fate would restore to grace to the archetype of Sleeping Beauty – all of them ethereal, on the rim of transcendence. I have no doubt that they crept into the deepest warrens of my psyche, leaving their delicate imprints thereafter; but yet inducing none of the miserable anxieties that physical self-consciousness brought into my soul a few years later.

At 7 or 8 or 9 identity is something locked away, waiting to be found. For me a feminine self was located in the future. In fantasies I conjured visions of myself at 15 or 16, dwelling on the bright details of appearance: a red drawstring bag, a check-patterned frock; I covered the pages of my drawing books with older 'me's: girls in pony tails and circular New Look skirts, ladies in fish tail evening dresses – all as curvy as fashion dictated at the time, with nipped-in waists and bulging breasts. Cradled by another kind of fantasy world, there were drawings of fairies and crinolines too.

With my teens, femininity turned into a pressing requirement; something was now expected of me. And this became a reason for shame and disgrace. I never felt, never believed that I looked feminine *enough*.

Physically self-conscious even at a younger age, I had still held some of the blithe confidence of anticipation: ugly duckling to swan. But the mirror seemed to deny it as I was confronted with the baleful image of my teenage self. Few others knew the agonies of my predicament: where they were round, as women should be, I was skinny and flat-chested. I would become glued to the mirror, contemplating these telling deficiencies of the flesh and, pulling my hair back from my face, I'd be gripped by the horrible certainty that it was *boyish*.

In a working-class culture that prized robustness and ample curves as measures of healthy feminine maturity, I had the misfortune to be mere skin and bone (women in the West of Scotland must have shrunk since the early 1960s, for the Glasgow shops are now crammed with the size 8s and 10s that I searched for in vain.) My 16–17-year-old body was an aberration, a freak of nature. Femininity eluded me and without its confirmation I was vexed with questions about who or what I was.

The banality of adolescent self-doubt; did other girls escape it? Some did, but I'm tempted to say: so what? when our difference from one another, our individuality and multiplicity of histories was partly at the source of our turmoil and sense of slipping selves, within a social reality where it was the difference *between the sexes* that was ordered, and set resolute patterns for living. Femininity has altered its meanings through history, but it is never absent from it, never outside the realm of the social and its divisions. And outside the social, where is the self?

Was I a real girl who would turn into a real woman? And Katherine Hepburn, with her elegant androgyny, her conquest of men by force of personality – did she soothe some of that troubled sense of identity? I would have been happy to be 'feminine' in that way, that was not all hips and bust and winsomeness. I would have been happy if I'd looked like *that*. If.

But troubled I was, and I think I've been haunted throughout adult life, by the ghost of those doubts. For paradoxically, to dispel the doubts by passing into adulthood and truly crossing the threshold of the sexually divided social order, is to invest a part of the self in social definitions of femininity. I am a woman. I reject the subordinate status accorded to women. At the same time femininity is stitched into my social being, and I distinguish myself as a woman by a variety of external behaviour, dress and decoration. I do not wish to be perceived *only* as a woman, nor do I wish to be perceived as *not* a woman.

The need for a 'feminine' sense of self isn't just something women can shake off with the conviction that it is false and imposed. We learned femininity in a world that assigned different roles and characteristics to girls and boys; but having acquired a social identity to which gender is integral, we are in no position to discard it at will. Identity is an intricate process of becoming, not an essential condition that is then overlaid with layers that can later be stripped away to reveal the true self. We are what we have become. The business of becoming someone else can never be total.

How easy is it, then, to create and keep an independent sense of self, when femininity is so much a part of that self, and when men so often have the power of confirming it or denying it?

Romance. Desire and erotic possibility. The narcissism that comes from a ceaseless anticipation of one's own image as it takes form in other eyes. The fragile determinations of physical identity. All of these can, by their very unfathomability, incline to contradict the rational formulations of autonomy written into women's present aspirations.

Since the eighteenth century, and the social and economic legitimation of the Englightenment's empirical philosophical systems, women's demands for equality have often had to rebut the idea of female incapacity for abstract thought and rationality (man as intellect: woman as emotions). In the more ambiguous views of human action and its motivations allowed by twentieth-century thought (neither man nor woman are entirely rational beings) there is room for women's demands to heed the promptings of irrationality. A recognition of how unconscious needs and compulsions shape sexual and emotional life, together with a social acknowledgment of women as active sexual beings, has led to contemporary feminism's avowal of the demand for sexual pleasure – and to the articulation of women's desire for and experience of such pleasure in all its diversity. This distinguishes contemporary feminism from earlier demands for women's liberation.[1]

But we live the past in constant conjugation with the present, where memory and the unconscious are concerned and where the contours of identity are concerned. And in all these we face the tortuous pathologies of desire. And we also live at a daily intersection of style and fashion and sexual imagery all suggesting the need for continuous transformations.

Contemporary feminist resistance to the tyranny of femininity – in those characteristics of appearance and decorum deemed appropriate for women – can be traced to the mythologised feminist protest at the 1968 Miss America Pageant. This was the famous 'bra-burning' seized on by the media. In reality no bras were burned, but to make the point that women's bodies were subjected by fashion convention to constrictive remodelling into the shapes that would please men, bras and girdles were symbolically thrown into a 'freedom trash bucket'.

Symbolic gestures matter; by ruffling the smoothness of the conventions that rule our lives, they can undermine what is taken for granted. They can also rebound, as this one so classically did, through a process of trivialisation that reduces the protest to no more than the gesture emptied of any but the most banal meaning; feminists as crackpot bra-burners.

But the gesture went further, and throughout the 1970s many active feminists wore their commitment as a visual statement that rejected the exaggerated sartorial trappings of femininity and the paraphernalia of artificial facial beauty. No (or little) make-up became *de rigueur* for feminists, and comfortable clothes had replaced constricting garments and high heels.

At women's movement conferences a feminist uniform became discernible: dungarees, worn with woollies in winter, baggy shirts or T-shirts in summer, lace-up boots or sandals, and no jewellery but for the plain silver insignia of women's symbol earrings. In 1976 I bought some denim dungarees, a red-checked cowboy-style shirt and some brown 'desert boots'; and for the next year or so this was the outfit I felt most comfortable in, with variations. It was my style.

This feminist style was a practical, less figure-hugging version of the casual unisex fashions introduced in the late 1960s, when jeans were everywhere. Each item in it had its provenance in the male wardrobe, but not only were these all items of *male* clothing, they were those of the manual worker. My outfit had all the connotations of tough physical independence, a kind of frontier serviceability. The style communicated a mood of militant determination not to be taken for granted as sex objects, not to be seen as frivolous, doll-like creatures dressed to fulfil a male idea or fantasy. Such a contrary stance towards the dictates of sex-role fashion and cosmetic beauty was truly exhilarating.

But fashion is artifice, and behind the sartorial rhetoric of intransigent practicality there was abundant compromise. My dungarees were a good deal tighter than some, I wore a touch of mascara, a dash of perfume, inscribing a feminine sub-text in my message of refusal to be forcibly feminised. I was not alone. Gender was only bent so far. With few exceptions the intention was not to communicate a total appearance of masculinity – to pass for a man – but to borrow from its visual vocabulary. Artifice in the service of honest artifice, not of spurious nature.

Fashion, which is constantly re-fashioned, depends on fluidity. Just as the fashion industry had looked to the styles of 1960s non-conformity for inspiration, so it captured the anti-femininity of feminism and reproduced it as sleek and glossy-bright glamour: clothes that were brazenly sexy, though still cut with comfort in mind. In pretty pastel or brilliant primary colours, in velvets and cords, satin and sheeny cotton, designer jump-suits retained the basic shapes of serviceability, but these were transformed and accessorised to the height of artifice. Likewise, with punk, a rebellion through style against the rigidities of fashion , in which make-up was worn as a flamboyant display of aggressiveness and clothes ranged from mocking bricolages of cast-offs and crim-polenes to the chains and leather of SM, style in its turn *became* fashion. The original impulses were acknowledged and claimed for mass consumerism. But there have been lasting gains, with a greater variety of fashion looks available to women and, as a result, a more knowing and creative use of fashion on the part of its consumers. As Angela Neustatter wrote in an *Observer* spread of articles on the changes wrought by the last decade of feminism,

> Most women now dress for themselves, opting for clothes which are comfortable and allow them mobility, no matter how bizarre and outré those clothes may be. If they don taffeta and glitter in the manner of Dallas and Dynasty it will be as self-indulgence, maybe even as parody. Most of all glorious individuality is the trademark of the young women of 1985; they make it impossible to imagine that the homogenous young women of the fifties will ever appear again.[2]

That spirit of fashion self-consciousness that denaturalises dress and makes it less an extention of some fixed form of femininity (however impermanent, for fashion has constantly altered the ideal feminine shape and appearance) and more a matter of slipping into one of several possible identity changes, owes a lot to the evolution of cultural criticism and its popularisation as well as to the impact of social mores on the rag trade. One of the first and most influential writers to deconstruct the meanings of modern style was the French theorist Roland Barthes. In Britain Angela Carter led the way for feminist analysts and commentators to set about interpreting the relationships between clothes and femininity. Some fashion journalists have in turn begun to explicate the cultural from the sartorial, and designers freely wield the rhetoric of parody, so that meanings become more and more involuted.

Clothes and their accoutrements are only part of how physical presence gives us gender definition. Our ideas about femininity and a sense of it as the core of physical identity are carved out of those idealised images that are internalised from childhood onwards – the remote universe of adult women and their masks, fantasy and the seductions of romance: sources of pleasure, or conduits to it. Pleasure is not to be disdained. Those aspects of femininity that are fun, creative or escapist are also offering the taste of what we lack or what we long for. In her collection of essays on different cultural representations of female desire and feminine pleasures – from fashion and food to ideal homes and television commercials – Rosalind Coward wrote,

> Female dissatisfaction is constantly recast as desire, as desire for something more, as the perfect reworking of what has already gone before – dissatisfaction displaced into desire for the ideal . . . .
> Our desire sustains us, but it also sustains a way of living which may not ultimately be the best and only way for women . . . . The pleasure/desire axis sustains social forms which keeps things as they are. The pleasure/desire axis appears to be everything women want but it may involve loss – loss of opportunity, loss of freedom, perhaps even loss of happiness.[3]

Our female pleasures and desires can offer confirmation and compensation, reassuring us about the attractiveness of our feminine selves and compensating for what is lost in that very confirmation. Through the pleasures of femininity we sustain ourselves, but if we make ourselves hostages to that femininity, we also risk surrendering the power to define ourselves in ways that do not accord with social (and male) expectations.

Femininity and masculinity are drawn into the structures of power that are the product of class and race hierarchies. In different cultures characteristics and forms of behaviour considered appropriately feminine or masculine can vary considerably, but they always mark off the boundaries of what is permissible for women and for men. A great deal is invested in superficial details of conduct and appearance: how we sit and move, the amount of space we occupy (much more for men, who are inclined to spread themselves physically while women tuck their bodies in and work at being neat and unobtrusive), our voices, our gestures, as well as bodily characteristics like smoothness or hairiness, muscularity or the lack of it. These secondary marks of gender are developed or acquired to a degree (men are hairier than women, but I shave my legs to accentuate that difference; I don't like being hairy). We have actively to maintain them. The fact that some lesbian women and homosexual men take a pride in not doing so, and in inverting the gender rules, is one reason why homosexuality is often so threatening to individual heterosexuals; by disregarding the rules they undermine their assumed naturalness.

If masculine and feminine roles are now less rigidly defined by codes of dress and appearance than they have been since the 1950s, and there's a tolerated anarchy of styles and looks that undercut or mock gender stereotypes, there has also been a proliferation of consumer spotlights on the body that accentuate gender. Since they first appeared in the early 1960s, teenage magazines have drawn for their readers a female body map of blemishes and defects, a topography of hair and nails and skin and teeth and hips and breasts that require a dedicated and intensive labour of maintenance and correction if the owner is to face the world in adequate feminine shape. Even a minimum programme of such attentions makes substantial claims on time and money.

The anxieties provoked by the continuous need to construct the feminine body and self are rooted in the contradictory implication of naturalness. What's suggested is that plump hips or hairy legs, skin that's flaky or nails that break, hair that's greasy (or dry or mousy) are *not* natural conditions, but regrettable individual aberrations from the true condition of femininity, to be remedied or else. The wounding and dispiriting impressions made by these early lessons in inadequacy linger on even to the age when the business of keeping up the body aesthetic (if not the body beautiful) is more a pleasurable and less an anxiety-inducing activity. The fact remains that it is the female body, not the male body, that is socially aestheticised.

In encouraging girls to enter traditionally male areas of

employment, the agencies concerned have had to emphasise the point that, contrary to stereotype, such jobs are not 'unfeminine'. Women entering craft apprenticeships over the last ten years or so (fewer than a dozen women were registered as apprentices in the construction industry in 1974) have often had to overcome the prejudices of employers and deal with workplace hostility, though as an increasing number of local authorities have adopted anti-discrimination policies and backed them up with active encouragement, the image of the woman plumber or carpenter has gained marginally greater visibility, and at the same time common sense ideas of what is acceptable as female employment have inched towards less fixed distinctions.

Young women's job choices and expectations often depend on notions of what is or isn't feminine. This is most marked in the case of school leavers going straight on to the job market with limited formal qualifications – into working-class jobs. There are clearly differentiated 'boys' jobs' and 'girls' jobs', when it comes to choosing between manual work where you get your hands dirty and service jobs where you don't. The apparent glamour of a boutique salesgirl's work and the less glamorous supermarket check-out job clearly have a more direct appeal for teenage girls whose outlook has been influenced by teen magazines, with their emphasis on consumer fashion and beauty, than does the prospect of construction work or electrical repairs, despite the fact that boys initially equipped with the same qualifications will have a trade, a skill and superior earning capacity within a few years because of their choice. (This is assuming, of course, that unemployment doesn't rule out the possibility of choice altogether.)

Built into the job choice without prospects that many young women make – for a combination of reasons and sometimes because there is no other choice – is an assumption, whether conscious or unconscious, about marriage in the near future. Contained in this assumption is the idea of dependency. In the most obvious sense this entails economic dependency, but consonant with this expectation is a set of other, quite different ones, that are nonetheless hard to separate from it: the husband as stronger, more capable, as someone who will take charge.

The reality rarely matches the vague expectation of secure male support for a family. The pattern is increasingly one of women's return to work after children have reached toddler-hood or school age (depending on child care availability), and this is usually work that has less status and pay than is available to women with more mobility and time. Whatever qualifications and training they do have are often irrelevant, given the limited job market available to women with young children. Despite the evidence of what the future might hold, it's hardly surprising that there's often a gap between young women's expectations that marriage will rescue them from the job market and the realities they must face. If the satisfactions of an interesting career or job achievement are not on the agenda it must make the illusions of domestic security all the more attractive.

This is where romance exerts its power. It features strongly in scenarios of male-female relationships in the worlds of teen magazines, and is a devouring preoccupation among adolescent girls. If you don't have a boyfriend you're missing out, and at the same time you lose status in the eyes of your peers, compulsively measuring success by the standards of feminine achievement. When I was 17 and in the sixth year at school one of my friends caused a stir of envy and swooning gasps of admiration when her boyfriend gave her a gold pendant engraved with the words, 'I love you today, more than yesterday and less than tomorrow.' Nothing could have seemed a more serious token of romantic involvement or a more earnest talisman for her protection. Gold, as they say in the advertisements, is for lovers. When you're 17 it comes at a price that banishes all threat of insecurity. To be loved by a man enough for him to lavish grown-up money on you, and one day to cover you with the mantle of all his worldly goods, is heaven indeed.

Romance conducts powerful female emotions, taming them into cliché. In its classic traditions women are literally swept off their feet. Men, of course, remain standing on theirs, no matter how enamoured they may be. The abiding image of romance fulfilled in these stories is of her enfolded in his arms (she delicate and slender against his craggy overpowering frame) as wedding bells pre-echo in the distance. The end is the beginning of a life in which she will be taken care of, inhabiting a timeless cameo of woman locked into a wished dependency. Romance is the promised haven of femininity.

Yet even the saccharine province of romantic fiction has been infused with a flavour of feminism. In the weekly women's magazines, between the covers of the Mills & Boons and the Harlequins, even in the newer teenage papers for girls, there are hints of rebellion, of women with spirit, behaving on their own terms. These jostle on the bookstalls with the perennial Barbara Cartland message that a woman's happiness lies in dedicated living for her man.

Although this is not a message that women can ever take to heart without a minimal dose of scepticism, its appeal is rooted in aspects of our emotional lives that do have an enduring hold. The essence of romance is the promise of being cared for, being special, being loved for who you really are, and being guaranteed a future of complete security.

In her book *Romantic Love and Society*,[4] Jacqueline Sarsby reports on the survey she carried out among several groups of teenagers on attitudes to love and marriage. The question about why people get married elicited quite different responses from boys and girls. Girls in all three schools where she conducted her research placed a much greater emphasis on 'security' as a reason for marrying. She quotes one girl: 'I think that women in particular get married for the security of a home and a husband to support them, although in this day and age marriage isn't necessary to gain security . . . .' As Sarsby herself points out, 'On paper, perhaps this is true – a woman and child need not starve alone, but the problems of a woman on her own are not just financial, as many of the girls realised. The desire to be needed, to matter to someone, was of prime importance to many of them.'

And what also emerged from one section of her study were two different pictures of men's needs and women's needs. Men's needs were seen on the whole as practical and domestic, and women's needs as emotional and financial. 'The picture was of marriage being a much more important emotional need for women than for men.'

To forsake femininity is to forsake that potentiality of a future in which needs will be met. But even for those of us who reject the mythic promises of romance and marriage, too much is at stake in any denial of the feminine self: pleasure, fantasy, an oneiric hoard of images, a repertoire of memories and recurring nostalgias glinting with the refracted possibilities of transformation.

Under a glass bell of synthetic memory, somewhere in High Society Land, Fred and Ginger dance together. Everything sparkles. The chandeliers send their chips of light through the iced crystal of the glasses, they gleam on the polished surface of the staircase that cascades down to the dance floor where couples sway to the Carioca. That's me in off-the-shoulder floor-length sequins; doors opened for me, cigarettes lit; the lady will have more champagne. Smiling, her admiring escort takes her hand and they dance, cheek to cheek, on the terrace that overlooks the moonlit bay. Night and Day you are the one.

Tinsel romance sustains us and betrays us, a tantalising mockery of longing, yet never to be despised for the longings and desires that it expresses. In the pulp romance of everyday, romance rewards femininity with symbiosis; the illusory security of the womb, the regained safety of arms that encircle and hold close, the bliss of merging with another. But in offering to women the lure of protection, the easy abdication of responsibility, it fashions an unequal symbiosis.

Why do women still accept this framework for relationships, with its predestined pattern of female dependency? Why do women who have achieved autonomy and self-definition in important areas of their lives, or have emerged from oppressive relationships with relief and enhanced perceptions, still hanker after the mirage of romance? Is it betrayal to take pleasure in femininity, to luxuriate in male attentions that acknowledge it, when we also wish to be acknowledged not only as feminine, and when the meanings of femininity are not just of our making?

Longings for what we never had? Recognitions that glimmered as we learned about sexual difference and its intimations of division and loss, eroding our spontaneous confidence, holding back the urge to explore the world of childhood without restraint, and beginning a split deep in the psyche that widened as we grew towards adulthood? What makes us so ambivalent towards our strengths? Is it that we live a paradox at the heart of female/feminine identity, so that by taking control of our lives we risk losing out on the most important things we learned it would bring to us?

CHAPTER 5

LIVING TOGETHER

JOANNA WATT

Joanna Watt is 34. She lives with Jim, with whom she has had a relationship for the past seven years, and their 1-year-old daughter Janie. Before Janie was born, Joanna and Jim had lived separately and had planned not to live together, except on a temporary basis after Janie's birth, on the principle that both could maintain their independence better that way, while spending time together and sharing childcare. With the arrival of Janie this became impracticable; after six months of parenthood they decided to give up the idea of separate households.

Both Joanna and Jim are teachers and have full-time jobs. They pay Jim's mother and sister-in-law to look after Janie while they are at work.

In Chapter 8 Joanna talks about her feelings and experiences as a mother. Here she talks about living together.

'I think certainly having a child makes quite a dramatic change to your life and what's possible. And for me that's been much more profound than actually living with a bloke or not.

'I think almost when Janie was born we were faced with the reality of the practicalities of looking after the child. I mean the idea of negotiating that, plus the relationship between me and Jim, and then to-ing and fro-ing between, particularly when I went back to work. It might have been possibly vaguely still on the cards [living separately] when I was on maternity leave. It's very difficult, because I think you put it down to practicalities, but obviously it is about a lot more than just practicalities.

I'm sure there are a whole lot of other elements in our relationship that made living apart difficult . . . we'd actually been through a lot of painful experiences in relation to having other relationships. I think probably having a child was part of all that, then living together was rationalised as being about practicalities.

'I'm quite surprised by it, because I'd rationalise why it was important for women to live apart from men and . . . I did want to live with a man, and in fact it's been a lot less tense and a lot less fraught, because in some ways my experience has been that all the things we fought for around being independent and being autonomous, have sort of crystallised around the idea of separate lives. In some ways my experience of that was actually more oppressive. Men could still play games, and could actually play them better, because you weren't so in touch with them, on a day-to-day basis.

'I don't feel that we are a couple in a way that immediately makes me think of a couple. We don't often have people round here together or go out together. In some ways I suppose we have more separate lives, paradoxically, now than we probably did when we were going out and seeing each other, because we would then spend the time together. Whereas now I do things separately a lot more than we do together – it's quite rare really. Even when we're here, because we've both got things to get on with, quite often we've been here and not actually spent that much time together. It's quite strange really. The thing that I expected to be more pressure for me has been less pressure.

Fighting for space

'I think if I were living with Jim without Janie then I would be fairly able to do largely what I wanted to do. But what does happen when you've got a baby is that – it's not just the baby, it's not just living with a man – it's like the two of those things coming together that make the difference. Even if you're both active, even if you're both doing things, there is still an underlying, quite often unspoken assumption that what *he*'s doing is more important. I feel I've always got to fight much more for my space than he has. I think he can – it probably sounds crazy, because his life has changed dramatically on the level of practicalities: he has to look after Janie, he has to do certain things for her – but on another level, a sort of psychological level, I don't think it's made nearly such a profound difference to him as to me. I still don't think that when a meeting comes up, or some evening thing to do with work, I don't think he immediately stops to think, "What about Janie?" Whereas that is always a presence for me. It just doesn't seem to be for him, although he would say that it is. I just feel that there is a whole set of dynamics under the surface . . . of course I haven't got the energy for battling, but it surfaces periodically that you have to fight for your space.

'On some levels you're sort of led to think that somehow housework has been sorted out, shouldn't be or isn't a problem any more. I find that encroaches on me a helluva lot more, and I feel almost guilty for saying that. I feel that if I was a right-on feminist I should have got rid of all those hang-ups about "I'm responsible". Jim's mother comes round, or someone who isn't part of the feminist consensus as it were – and I immediately feel the responsible person. When I'm trying to work I find it really difficult to just cut off from that. I find it difficult to cut off from the practicalities of Janie and getting things prepared for her. I also find it difficult to cut off from the fact that somewhere needs cleaning or somewhere's in a mess. Those things really do encroach, and if you talk about independence those things really do encroach on it. And make it really quite difficult for us to be independent in our lives. Single-minded in our pursuits, right? Things that are important to us.

'I find it quite a relief that I no longer work with Jim

[they used to teach in the same school]. I think it was more difficult for me to be self-defining in a context where he was actually in the same work situation and quite powerful and quite articulate. I think that made it hard for me sometimes. I also find it very good that we have separate political lives, because no one round here sees me in relation to him at all, and they actually perceive *me* as the activist, and *he's* just this person sort of in the background. Whereas if he were in the Labour Party here, or I there, where he works, then that would quite panic me. Apart from the women's groups at the school when we were teaching, it was very difficult for me to carve out a space for myself, and I suspect it would be still. I would *feel* it as a difficulty if we were in the same Labour Party branch. He's talked about moving to this one and I feel quite resistant to it – even though he would make a good contribution. I just really enjoy the fact of being seen as *me*, and nothing to do with Jim at all. And he does have a particularly sort of heavy, straight-down-the-line approach, which always leaves no room for doubt, so if you have got doubt then the danger is you'll get carried along with his certainties, when you actually might be full of doubt yourself. That's really important to me.

Double standards

'I think living together takes the focus off being in love. You know, being in love is sort of like the lynch-pin of your relationship, which again I find quite a relief. It's just there, it's not the sort of mover in quite the way that it was beforehand.

'I think in some ways at an emotional level I probably felt more dependent on Jim before we lived together than I do now. I probably felt more panicky about it, because it was something that was always under discussion and negotiation, and constantly sort of moving and changing, and . . . quite threatening I suppose, which I don't feel

in the same respect now. I don't feel so much that I've
been manipulated; I just feel that he has an inability to
face up to situations. I can see quite easily a situation
where he could get involved with someone else but
couldn't face up to negotiating that with me, but prefers
to run away from it and conduct it in a secretive fashion.
I find it quite an interesting comparison living with Jim
as compared to living with Jeff that I lived with a few
years ago. He would never say that he wasn't one of those
macho men – in many ways he wasn't that conscious
about sexism, but somehow he was naturally more
egalitarian. I suppose he didn't have such an ego as Jim's
got. I suppose that's what it comes down to.

'Some of the difficult things only came up around sexual
jealousy, and given that we don't at the moment have
other sexual relationships, it sort of seems to be better.
But that was the thing that really used to annoy me more
than anything else, whatever was said at the rational,
theoretical level. I mean the whole double standard that
was at work, and also interesting is the way in which
jealousies are expressed by male and female. His was
much more of a sort of enraged acting out in a very
aggressive way, whereas mine was much more sort of
internalised hurt. . . .

Equal parents?
'All the women I've talked to who have recently had kids,
have all said the same thing. They've all said, "Yes he
does all the things that I do; changes the nappies and
gives the kid a bath and so on, but he does not have the
overall responsibility in the way that we feel it." And
clearly we can't just say that's the male problem. I mean
it says something about how we experience motherhood
and our expectations about it. And that's what's draining
me. Because sometimes I think I shouldn't *be* so tired, but
when I think about it I think that's what it is: all the
time feeling that you're the person who is ultimately

responsible. And quite often I don't go to things just because I feel that I just want to get some time on my own. It's puzzling, because Jim just doesn't seem to have that; it's not a problem for him. The way it tends to come out – it can come out in general discussion, but often it comes out when I'm most tired, and just get upset, and it all comes out in a great big rush, like it's been building up over a period. But for all that I feel I'm very different from my mother, I can see patterns of her in me. I see her as a very strong woman. Of the two people I would see her as the driving force, between my father and my mother. But in terms of getting upset and housework, there's a whole series of things that I still find it very difficult to break out of.

'And in terms of independence, it's not just you and your relationship. It's actually the source of insecurities and worries and the pattern is really deeply ingrained, ways of handling situations which do go into very predictable patterns. I can see that at an objective level, but I still find it very difficult to stop going along those grooves.

'There was a terribly difficult period, just before him moving in with me. What came out of it was just how terrified he was of me leaving, and that was an absolutely terrible fear. There would be a great aggressive to-do and then he would crumble. But even when he was crumbling it was still in a power-trip way. Somehow it didn't feel like the woman traditionally crumbling, it just felt like an act of control. I can remember one night clearly, that was probably the worst point in my relationship with him. It was when he was seeing someone else and didn't tell me, and then I found out as it was ending. It was just as he moved in that it all came out, and I just felt absolutely angry. I was totally freaked out, I felt extremely vulnerable, I felt very unable to be independent. That was also bound up with feeling sexually unattractive; that was quite salutary for me, because of how much my sense of self was bound up with what I looked like. Perhaps one shouldn't be surprised at that, but it does pose it very acutely when you're pregnant, and no one can actually perceive you as other than a pregnant woman. I was just absolutely upset, enraged, furious.

'I went to stay with a friend that night. He insisted on driving me round there, then did this whole crumbling act in the car, by the end of which I felt guilty and as if I'd been horrible. It's all the things about being a woman and being sympathetic and being understanding and comforting. But even that wasn't straightforward and I got quite cross with myself, because bloody hell, why was I furious? And by the end of it I started to feel not so much furious as very upset. Upset and hurt and so on. I also did manage to keep the absolute fury, and yet somehow that just gets dissipated by this little boy act: "I can't cope without you" sort of thing. And I think the way he justifies it is because his relationship with me is the important thing, but he wants his cake and wants to eat it at the same time . . . and he doesn't want to face up to the implications of what he's doing, he doesn't want to give me the power to behave in the same way as him, because that could then threaten him.'

At this end of the north London street where I live, with front doors discreetly closed on private dramas, it's traditional family life that spills outside. Families are what are most visible, most audible: cars coming and going, babies and toddlers bundled in and out of them along with the paraphernalia of childhood; human traffic in twos and threes, voices and other busy sounds that reverberate across the narrow space between the tall buildings. A few gaping open-plan basements reveal youngish women in the motions of kitchen chores. Men are to be seen earnestly intent on car washing, digging the garden, stripping paintwork or with dripping brushes in hand.

The very gregariousness and home-centred character of family life among (mostly) owner-occupying couples and their children make single lives all the more muted: marginal and invisible in the purposeful identity of such a street. If you live alone it sometimes seems as if the whole world's in a nuclear family: the whole world but you. (It isn't: only a small minority of households in Britain conform to that standard model.)

At this end of the street there are two women – that I know of; there are bound to be others – running their own cars and their own mortgages, busy with their own networks of friends and relationships. Another lives just around the corner. How far their single lifestyles are a matter of choice or circumstance, it's impossible to know. Whichever it is, like all single women below a certain age they have to contend with the way the world looks at them, as women living without men. Perhaps it is disapproval, perhaps envy, perhaps the superiority of the smug, or sheer 'neighbourly' nosiness about what ostensibly unattached women get up to. Family life is taken for granted; other lifestyles make you think twice.

Where the Victorian terrace comes to an end on one side of the road, there's a borough council laundry, great wads of curling steam issuing from its ducts and skylights. Inside, women from the council blocks that stretch down to the far end of the street do family washes. Ten or twelve massive machines whirr and swish, perpetually in motion, and there's usually a queue waiting to use them. Women often come in twos and threes: mothers and daughters, sisters, maybe sisters-in-law. Children play together. On the whole, the atmosphere is courteous and cooperative, with neighbours and strangers helping to fold sheets or feed them into the hot ironing rollers, and people chatting desultorily as they keep an eye on the progress of the wash cycle. The laundry's an informal multicultural meeting place, with its inner-city mixing of black and white, African and Afro-Carribean,

Asian and Turkish Cypriot. It's cheaper and nicer than any tacky commercial launderette. I used to go there, before I owned a washing machine. But I don't miss humping my laundry there and back, I don't miss heaving the loads in and out of machines and extractors and driers, or the time it wastes.

Beside the self-contained domestic privacy of middle-class life (which easily encompasses the idea of individual independence) there are remnants of working-class mutuality and interdependence, values that continue because people have a need for them. It is not hard to see why more money and a greater degree of choice may render them dispensable. The narrowness of our society makes anonymity and self-sufficiency acceptable refuges from the insistent nudgings of respectability.

Daily life in the mid-1980s is pervaded with the unease that comes from social panic and economic desperation, whether relayed long distance or faced at close quarters. Yet it still carries the long echoes of an era of radical optimism that envisaged personal change as an intimate part of political transformation. The changes were to be undertaken fearlessly, breaking with the old through alternative lifestyles that promised exciting, unknown freedoms: communal living, squatting, open relationships, non-monogamy. All of these implied some combination of interdependence and independence: they also implied risks, but the invisible safety net of material social progress was there. Now that it's gone, the demands of necessity override the dangerous romance of flagrant optimism. For many hopeful radicals the obstacles to change had already proved greater than imagined; the tenacity of the old had been underestimated, as had its grip on individual psychic structures and on larger social ones.

One example of this is the way in which family memories and emotions resonate through the dynamics of communal living arrangements. Looking back on a long experience of alternative households, in 1983 Wendy Clark wrote in the feminist collection *What Is To Be Done About the Family?*,

We enter the family as children and we leave it as adults, and it is what happens, or what we *think* should have happened, that we are always trying to recreate or recast. It is not just alternative domestic arrangements, new childcare forms of sharing household tasks – we are also constantly searching for the less tangible aspects of what it all means to us. And we constantly become confused by the reality and the ideal. Whenever I feel depressed, I think of home and family; whenever another woman thinks of home and family, she becomes depressed. It is contradictions like this that prevent the alternative households we create from working for as long and as effectively as we would like.[1]

And a few years earlier, Denise Riley, arguing against the oversimplification of 'sexism and the family' as mere ideological mystifications and misperceptions, underlined their solid material reality:

Around 1968 I used to assume that the family was to do with R.D. Laing conceptually and also something that had almost got me: and then I miraculously escaped from it into some ageless revolutionary zone, as it were. But now, as a single mother, I'm rather well placed to see that the family is omnipresent in every social structure of capitalism, that it is not left behind us in our painful histories, that it is in front of us, and to one side of us, and the *raison d'être* of, and the assumption behind, most social and economic and legislative institutions. Even at the level of State-defined poverty, 'benefits' are predicated on the family structure of one wage-earner and home-labourer, rigidly defined by gender.[2]

We are irremediably social beings, our daily lives grounded in the persistent realities of old values and old feelings even as we falteringly move to escape them. The safety of belonging in a subculture can soften the asperities of marginality, of trying to transform your personal life in opposition to a culture whose dominant values and social forms clash continually with yours. Where the subculture itself loses its coherence, self-reliance is more than ever called for. The retreat to the family and to traditional lifestyles that has been so ruefully noted by many feminists and socialists in recent years has taken place in the context of widespread economic insecurities and social restrictiveness. If the wolf is at the door you don't unlock it, and even those untouched directly by the hardships of unemployment, falling living standards or housing shortages, can't but feel more vulnerable, and impelled to dig in and hang on to what they have.

' . . . all the things we fought for around being independent and autonomous, have sort of crystallised around the idea of separate lives,' observes Joanna Watt. And it's the very difficulty of separate lives for women that has made support and validation so important. At the same time women are also struggling with these problems – how to maintain a core of independence and autonomy – within the couple, living with a man. It is not surprising that many women desire closeness and daily connectedness with a lover; in western industrial society not only is the single woman cast as an outsider, but the exclusiveness of household units often means that the couple or family is the only place where certain emotional needs can be met, and where practical interdependency can grow, where there's warmth and the sharing of news and ideas, meals cooked and eaten together, small treats and indulgences, and the sense of fun and playfulness that can only be released by relaxed intimacy.

Of course the couple too is troubled by the echoes of family histories and expectations, as well as by old habits and attitudes to the sexual division of labour – even where these are consciously contested. In engaging with the ideal of equal partnership women are obliged to confront themselves as much as the men they are with. The pressures on the woman in the couple are even greater where there are children or where the traditional economic imbalance prevails, with the man earning more or regarding his work or career as primary. At the same time single status is less of an option for those working-class women who are most vulnerable to traditional sexual divisions because of their low earning power.

Some women choose not to live with men because they see it as the only solution to the conflicts of the couple; some women long for the shelter of coupledom, and see being single as something to be made the best of. Both groups may see the woman who is married or living with a man as socially privileged, and they are correct in this perception.

When I decided to move in with a man after several years of living on my own one woman friend reacted by telling me she saw it as a betrayal, a capitulation to the social norm. Every woman who gave up her independence to form a heterosexual couple was, she argued, undermining the already precarious status of other more resolute women. I had some sympathy with her view, although a 'separate life' was not something I had ever resolved on as a principle. But it's how I feel about marriage. Another friend was convinced we'd be less close; I'd be less available and we'd have less in common. I'd felt the same in the past about others, and about women friends having their first child.

The couple absorbs energy and time, but the domestic disappearing trick is less likely, less frequent now that female friendships matter more than ever, their emotional richness fostered by years of re-evaluation. If you enter the couple with no illusions about its simplicity, with the knowledge or the fear that its intimacies can lead to loss of definition as they peel away layers of protective skin and dissipate boundaries, then the need to hold on to other connections is vital. Friendship is a mutual necessity as well as a social pleasure and a source of other joys. The insights and support of friends nourish the strengths shaken by dependency, although delicate manoeuvres may be required to skirt the territory of doubt that separates friends shut out by a wall of domestic togetherness, and by the settled comforts of the home it encircles.

Behind the grim failure of radicalism conjured by the 1980s' 'retreat to the family', some of the fruits of change remain. The very multiplicity of family forms, and their multicultural character, rocks the complacency of the old familial icons. With small changes in confidence, women are more likely to press their own demands on family structures, even as some women find greater responsibilities pressed on them. Change filters across the social divide and the margins have shifted in places, letting new ideas and ways of living slip in.

Since the nuclear family in the nuclear age came into the shadow of disrepute, it's become a little less of a prison for those who suffer its worst distortions of power. A few escape routes have been opened: battered women's refuges; self-help mechanisms for parents under strain and the children threatened by them; support for incest victims. All have been created out of the demands and priorities of the women's movement.

For the woman who rejects old patterns and mythical certainties, whether consciously as a feminist or in a spontaneous spirit of dissatisfaction, there are no guarantees in the couple and no easy accommodations. For her and the single woman alike it's a matter of living with the difficulties of change. We all have to improvise.

Sometimes at night family violence crashes into the sleeping street. Male and female sexual insults are screamed, in-laws reviled, anger roared to a frenzied crescendo that simultaneously orchestrates the listening silence in every nearby house. All of us lying in our beds, grateful for our private tranquillity; everyone keeping *their* secrets.

By coincidence, the writer Sheila Macleod set her novel *Axioms* – about the break-up of a marriage and a family – in this very street, just across the road.

Claire Booth   Claire Booth is 38. She has two chil-

dren, aged 2 and 3. She was married for five years. When her second child was born she gave up her job as a full-time lecturer, aiming to continue with some part-time work and income from private tuition in her own home. Soon after, she separated from her husband.

In chapter 7 she talks about her feelings and experiences as a mother. Here she talks about living alone.

'It quite worries me about ever settling down with somebody. I think to myself that another person would actually be much easier. But I feel a great simplicity in my life. Especially with children it's much easier, even though the whole burden of them goes on in your own head — but then you can get quite a lot of advice from other people. I'd have to negotiate a different set of feelings. I sometimes feel that although my life's been difficult and complicated, separating was the great simplifying factor in it.

'The minus side is that it's so lonely. Although there are good friends and good support and good family, of course I still feel lonely. I'm never quite sure whether this is the moment I'd want to settle down with somebody, but if I think in the long term of never being with somebody, I don't like that idea at all.

'It's paradoxical. On the one hand if I hadn't been so strong I couldn't really have survived what Peter made me carry. On the other hand if I'd been much stronger I wouldn't have put up with it, in a way. Partly because I was so dependent I didn't say, "Oh, this is ridiculous, I'm not going to carry on with it much longer; apart from anything else I've got enough self-respect not to carry on with this." There's no doubt there was a large part of me that stayed with him because I wanted to have children. But I managed to look after him and look after myself, to take all the responsibility, emotional responsibility, which is what I think a lot of women do. But if I had perhaps been stronger and had felt better

about myself, and more confident about my ability to
be with a man, then I might not have tolerated living with
him.

'I think there's such a thing as strong women who end
up in their own traps. I think strength can be a trap.
You don't allow yourself to be weak, perhaps because
you feel so weak, and you develop a sort of strength and
independence. Maybe from very young you're brought up
to be excessively self-controlled and self-dependent, but
really underneath you've been forced into that situation.
I was the oldest in my family, and then I went to
boarding school. You learn to live up to your parents'
expectations so much that you develop a tremendous
strength. It's based on shoring yourself up quite a lot.

'I'm not being drained by Peter any more. And I'm not
being upset and distressed by him. I am being drained
by the children to a certain extent, but that's a much more
natural kind of relationship, a necessary kind of
relationship. I felt a lot of resentment towards him, which
is very draining. I don't feel that same kind of resentment
towards the children. I know they need to grow through
dependence into independence. Peter couldn't; he needed
to become a grown-up man, which is very different from
a child.

'I think if I had another relationship I would want
monogamy. It wouldn't be the end of the world if he
went off and spent the night with somebody, but I
wouldn't want to be living with him if this person was
being seen regularly. There may be people who can
give each other that kind of freedom all the way round,
but it's just too hard work for me. It's possibly a lot
different when you're much younger. If I were to have
another relationship I don't want it to be fraught with
all sorts of problems. And there are problems, whatever
you think things *should* be. They are emotionally very
wearing.'

YVONNE HUGHES Yvonne Hughes has remarried
recently after several years living alone with her children
following divorce. She is 42.

'I was happy being independent and on my own –
although when you've got children you're never totally
on your own anyway. You feel that you're a failure in a
sense because you don't come up to the super-image of
a woman. But it's almost impossible, because when you're
working, doing a full-time job and trying to cope with
controlling teenagers – there's much more of a strain on
you, because of the environment of high unemployment
you worry so much about the future of your grown-up
children. I think it's a real strain.

'Sharing it with somebody helps in a sense because
when I was on my own, when I made a decision
regarding the children I used to feel scared that I'd made
the wrong decision, because I felt that they were my total
responsibility, and if things went wrong it would be my
fault. I don't feel quite as much the same now, although
really my husband doesn't make decisions for my children
– they're too grown-up anyway for him. And I wouldn't
accept his decisions really – by someone who's not their
father.

'I'm the first of a family of four. Being the eldest makes
a difference to your outlook anyway. You're the first
and expectations are quite high of you. I was told that
I'd been put on a pedestal – my mother made quite a
lot of me, maybe because my father was in the war, in
the army, when I was born. I didn't really cause her too
much hassle, because I had a brother who was three years
younger and he got up to all the tricks, so I think I sort
of behaved myself more. I think I grew up to be fairly
responsible. Plus, my mother wasn't very good at
managing money. And my father was a little bit mean

with money. She worked. She worked as we got older, she never sort of stayed at home all the time.

'I've always lived in the East End. I've never moved. My father still lives in this area. My mother died when she was 43. I had two children when she died, I mean my son was only 2 months old, and that was one of the cornerstones in my life that went. It was a real sort of mother and daughter relationship. It was quite strong. So I think at the time I missed her, because the children were young, and they weren't going to have a nan. She would have been what I call a real nan. She would have looked after them and bought them all the presents, and really sort of spoiled them I suppose. And I used to cry quite a lot thinking that my children would miss out of her kind of loving, because she was really quite a special person. I used to get really down because of her going. So I had to tell myself that she would be really angry with me because I had two children to look after and was responsible for them. It was one of the things that used to make me lose it and get on with life. I'd never lost anyone before, and I think when you lose your mother it's one of the hardest. Most women are the mainstay of the family. When the mother goes or dies the family sometimes breaks up.

'It's funny really, she was the one who did the light fittings, she was the one who did the decorating, because she had to, because my father wasn't very good. And she believed that girls should be educated. I mean I know it's not *that* long ago, but when I was 15 it wasn't considered so important for girls to be educated, as well as boys. But my mum thought it was important, and she wanted me to be.

'I thought it was because she was a bit of a dunce at school. She was very clever in lots of other respects, but she wasn't very clever at school, so that sort of made her want me to have a good education. She encouraged me, but she couldn't help me, but I would have her support,

with school. I can't remember my father being very
interested in it really. It was her mostly. And I think in a
way I failed her expectations, because when it came to
leaving school I stayed on till I was 16 and took my O-
levels, but I used to worry quite a lot about exams. I
got, I think, 2 O-levels, but when it came to job and
career it was a totally different ball game, because the
kind of O-levels that I got wasn't good for the kinds of
jobs that I was interested in. And when I was at school,
when we used to have the Christmas parties and things,
I'd take over the organising of catering. I was always in
the group that did things in the class, I always used to
get involved in loads of things. I remember my teacher
saying, "She should go into catering," and my mother
was most annoyed – "You're not becoming a waitress."
I never really became what I intended to be, I just ended
up . . . I did a hairdressing apprenticeship for about three
months and hated it. I wanted to be a beautician.

'Then I went into Boots the chemist, and then I became
a chemist's assistant and I did that for quite a long while.
And I got married at 19. I had my daughter before I was
21. It was a real disappointment – I mean I didn't want
to be a mother that young – disappointed that I became
pregnant quite so quickly. I was angry. I mean, it's funny
really, because you're quite naive – and my husband said
it would be OK, and it wasn't OK. So she was an
accident, and really and truly I hadn't intended to have a
family for four or five years; that was *my* idea. I really
wasn't ready for motherhood – because I went back to
work six weeks after I had her, because I felt I had my
own identity at work. I've always preferred to work and
be my own person in that sense, rather than just be a
mother and a wife. I find that's not enough for me really.

'You don't really know yourself that well, do you, when
you're a teenager. I can remember my schoolmistress
saying to me that if ever there'd been a need for a
suffragette, I would have been one. So I must have been

– well, I didn't hold boys in such high esteem; I wasn't one of those who thought that boys were sort of wonderful, or men were wonderful. And I used to argue I think quite strongly in class when we had discussions, and I wasn't terribly interested in having babies. It's really quite funny when I look back, because . . . well I often think that I lost control, that I was as much in control of my life as I would like to have been, but then when I was I still didn't control it very well. It's not that simple. I mean some people say they can do something, and I often believe that fate and other things often prevent you from doing the things that you sometimes want to do.

'It's very difficult, it's such a big conflict. I think where I was different even I suppose in school – I was the only girl who took science and the only girl who took physics. And I can remember I came top. Just once. And the teacher turned around to the boys and said; "You can't let a girl beat you." And I think if I'd been more aggressive or more determined I would have tried to prove him wrong.

'I get very angry in my body every month, because it feels so uncomfortable, and I'd like to be able to take myself out of it, and remove myself from it. And men don't have that kind of problem. When you're very young it does have an effect on you, even though you're not aware of it.

'I remember becoming aware that I was growing up about 15, because boys started taking an interest in me. And I think between 15 and 16 what I really should have been doing was studying and concentrating on schooling, and I was discovering that life could be a giggle and fun, and it came at the wrong time. I know with my son and my daughter, the age when they start waking up to the idea that life can be enjoyable and they can have a real good time is the time when they should be sitting indoors studying and working hard. Girls are fine at school until they start getting to the age when other things happen to them.

'I think why I got married so young was, you know, the strong feelings that you get when you're in that age group. I met my first husband, and I think it was more a physical thing rather than any emotional thing, and nobody tells you the kind of feelings that you can go through – like you're sort of plodding along and you're quite happy, then all of a sudden you're in this age group, and there's all these feelings churning away. If I'd grown up now, with contraceptives and much freer attitudes, I probably wouldn't have felt the need to marry like I did then. Nice girls didn't then. Girls didn't have sexual feelings then, they weren't supposed to feel anything. If you wasn't a nice girl then nobody wanted to know you. I don't think it was really true even then, but that was the kind of pressure. And it's still even now. I mean I've got a daughter who's 19 and I'd hate to think she was just being indiscriminate in her relationships – I think that it is more damaging just to sleep around. It doesn't do you much good as a person.

'I had two children before I was 24. My son was planned, because I went back to work and worked for a while. I think if I hadn't gone back to work I might have had him sooner. But I went back to work and I had my own independence again. My mother looked after my daughter for a while and also a very good sister-in-law who had one the same age. And what happened was when I had my son and I was at home she went back to work, so we helped one another.

'Both my children went to nursery, but it was at 3; you couldn't get them in before 3, unless you paid, and then it wasn't much point working, because it would have cost so much. The wage I earned wasn't that great that I could afford it. I think I preferred the family.

'I got divorced in the thirteenth year of my marriage. I can remember after ten years thinking, oh god, I'm not happy, but it was easier to stay in it. I think if he hadn't become – he was a gambler, so that I found difficult. I mean I had to work really, to be able to keep up; I couldn't rely on him for money. But I think if I hadn't found out that he'd been unfaithful to me, that he'd found someone else, I probably would have stuck it, I would have stuck out for the marriage, even though the gambling was – I don't know, it's hard to say. I was unhappy and I decided; I remember thinking, well the marriage is no good, so perhaps I can find a job that will occupy me so that it won't matter so much that the marriage wasn't so good. And I was thinking of doing a teacher training course at one time, but I lacked the confidence. I'd got to the point when I didn't believe in myself any more and so I didn't have the push to do it.

'I was still working in the chemist's, and I was doing a bit of dispensing. I used to run the shop, so I was like a manageress, and I used to enjoy the work. I was getting divorced when I was made redundant. And that was terrible, that was really awful, because while I was getting divorced as long as I could go to work and keep up the normal functions I was OK. But when that was taken away from me I just broke up I think. But then I thought, well I can't stay at home because I'll go barmy, too much time to think, so I joined a course. A playgroup course. And while I was there I did a women's study group and an English class, and took an O-level. So I got quite involved.

'I went on to actually work in a playgroup for a while, but only part-time because I was on social security. I decided not to go back to work properly because I felt that my children needed me to be more around. I wanted to be there when they came home, because I was very much aware that I had to be their mainstay after what had happened. I was really worried about the effect on them. But I think it's better to have one parent that's stable than two that keep arguing, so that was one of the reasons.

'You learn a lot about other people, going through that,

but you also learn a lot about yourself. You find that you're much more vulnerable to making mistakes. You have to be more liberal, because you're actually forced to be more liberal. You discover things about yourself that you didn't have to think about when you were married. I mean if you're married for a long time – I was married nearly thirteen years – well you get used to just being *married*, and you don't think about anything else. And all the sort of things like your friends don't invite you round because you're on your own, you don't like telling people that you're divorced because they think you might – it's so true to form. Widows also suffer the same problem.

'I can remember being petrified of actually going into a pub and having a drink with a friend, because it was OK for a man to have a drink with a friend, but if a woman went in with a friend it meant she was on the look-out, or she wanted to be picked up. I mean socially it's much easier to be a couple than it is to be single, for a woman. Maybe it's hard too for single men, but I don't think it's as hard as it is for a single woman.

'It was difficult being on my own anyway, because of – I'm not very confident sexually about myself. I felt so ugly and unattractive. The personality was given quite a shock. I can remember I made sure that I went out every morning not looking like a poor cow. I didn't want people saying, oh look, poor girl, he's left her, look at her now. I used to go the other way, I used to stink of perfume, you know really sort of make my face up, put on a mask almost – that's what it was like for me, because inside I felt so brittle. But I put on this face and I thought I'm not going to let those bastards know how unhappy I am. I mean they must have known that I tried not to let it show in that respect.

'It was only when I became involved in the playgroup – it was really marvellous – there were lots of women who were on their own, and we became very supportive with one another. And that's when you see the different side of how women react, to being on their own. I had always thought that women were always the goodies, and that men were always slightly inferior. And I discovered that no women are the best, kind of thing, and that's when I discovered how really different lots of people are. When you're mixing with a group of women who're mostly single, that's when you know. Some were quite casual, promiscuous, about relationships, and I used to find that quite amazing. That's when I think I started growing up a bit to the facts of life.

'Round here a lot of people don't particularly approve of divorce. It's still, "You've made your bed, lie on it," kind of thing. They still find it fairly difficult to accept. . . . But sometimes when my son gets very angry, even now, about it, I feel guilty from the hurt that he's had. My mother stayed in a marriage that was fairly heavy for her, and I felt, "Well you could stick it out for so many more years, but there's not so many years left for you" and I thought, "I'm not going to do it." So in a way she was responsible for me doing it but in a sort of . . . the opposite really.

'It was not that hard for me to be on my own, because I'd actually been on my own for quite a while; I was left on my own quite a bit. Financially I wasn't dependent on him, because of him being a gambler, so I'd to manage on my money anyway. So in some respects he prepared me for being alone, if you like, because I felt very much on my own anyway. The marriage wasn't my idea of what a marriage should be.

'The thing was the security. I've got married again and I feel much happier now. I don't feel threatened any more if you like. I was on my own for seven or eight years. I mean I could cope quite well for long periods of time being totally on my own, but if I was to go into a relationship I found I couldn't handle the kind of reaction I sometimes found in myself. Because I think I'm quite a warm person, and a loving person, and I had to stamp on all those feelings in a sense, and that I found difficult.

'I think if I could have handled that – because of the working-class background – if I could have handled the fact that I could have a little more than a cuddle every so often, and some affection, I could have stayed on my own, I could have been on my own. But I couldn't handle that kind of attitude, because I was brought up to believe in marriage. I mean people wonder why I've married again, when I could have just easily lived with someone, but if I was going to live with him it had to be total commitment. And also because I couldn't do that to my children, because I wanted to give them security, and I wouldn't have felt secure. It's very complex really. I mean you don't even know why you're doing a thing. I think a lot of the time it is social. It is easier. From society's point of view it makes it just easier to be a couple rather than on your own.

'And I think I used to worry such a lot about being regardèd as a problem family. You become a problem family because you are actually a single-parent family, and that I found very difficult. If you like, the spotlight's on you, people know a lot about you and your children, whereas if you're in a secure family it doesn't seem to matter. And I think also this thing about cohabitation. I used to hate the thought that maybe I would be watched, or observed to see if I was cohabiting. Once I remember I put some shirts on the line. They were my father's, and I thought I wonder if they'll think – I couldn't stand that side of it all. I was much happier being at work and having a job that I can do.

'I've only been married since April last year. I was working for over two years in full-time employment before that. I'd worked part-time in the library. I also did another course, a two-year course in sociology, English and art. It was part-time. That was great; I really enjoyed that. Really and truly I've grown a great deal since my divorce. My first husband was the type who was jealous, and he wouldn't let me go anywhere. I used to fight at the beginning, and then near the end. I really resented the fact he never trusted me, and he was the one who was doing all the things. I wanted to go to evening classes.

'I loved the freedom. It was great. I don't regret leaving. It's benefited me as a person.

'I had a very supportive family – my sister and my father – and I had friends who were supportive; friends of my own, not friends of our marriage. I'm very much a woman's kind of person really; I tend to trust women far more than I would trust men.

'I got involved with the community centre where I work. Because you've got the time to do it you throw yourself into those things.

'Fortunately, in this marriage I've got a husband who trusts me and I can still make decisions and I don't get hassled the way I was in the previous marriage. . . . There's much more an equal relationship. I found it difficult, I still find it difficult – any relationship is difficult – but so far it seems to be working.

'What I miss is that I can't see my women friends the way I used to. I miss that. I'm not saying I can't see my friends, I just can't do it as often. And some of my friends' husbands work of an evening, and that was fine, you know, it was just us. But if I decide to go somewhere sometimes, I can't really just leave my husband on his own. And I've found that friends I've had for an awful long time and I've known their husbands, it changed when I got married, because it upset the balance of the friendships. That's one thing, because the friendships that you've had for a long time when you were on your own you can't continue to the same degree. Because you don't need to make the effort, sometimes you don't.

'Because I'm married, if I go into a group where there are lots of men, I don't feel threatened, because I'm married. And I think, well I really would like to know more about why I feel like that, and I think that when I wasn't, I used to feel spare. It's a positive feeling, because you've not become different outwardly, but inwardly you feel so different.

'It always seems to feel a more sexual overtone if you're single than when you are married. But in actual fact sometimes because you're more relaxed you are more sexually attractive.

'I find that I very much have been domesticated, but it angers me sometimes that I have so. I feel like someone who is playing a role that's expected of me, rather than doing the role from the heart.

'I work full-time. But I think I tend to do more of the domestic things. Because I worked full-time and did it anyway before. I find I get a bit more help now than I did when I was on my own. One of the nice things was when I was sick – you know when you're not well and to actually go to bed and have someone look after you is really nice. Whereas before, that didn't happen. It's a much more comforting feeling to actually be looked after again. I think it is nice to have some of the responsibility taken off you. Bills I don't have to worry about, because we've got this arrangement that I buy the food and he does all the bills. And it works quite well, because I don't have to worry.

'It's funny, there are quite little things. Like different radio programmes. He used to come into the living room in the morning and I'd have one programme on and he used to switch it over to another one, because that's what he wanted to listen to and because he'd always done that. Silly little things, but they can be quite hard to cope with.

'Actually I don't think the little bit of paper really makes . . . I think a relationship does. I always think marriage is a convenience for society; it's really to do with property and such. I think a person is married if they're

in a one-to-one relationship and they're working on it.
That to me is a marriage.

'I think you still have to give way on certain things. I
think you either have to keep fighting, and then you
wear yourself out, or you have to slip sometimes more
into the accepted world. I do, I slip back into my
accepted role, and then I get angry with myself, and then
I shout and moan and scream that I'm not going to be
like this. And then. . . .

'When I look back sometimes I think I wish I could just
have a chance to just be me, for a little while, rather
than being what I became. You know instead of becoming
a mother so quickly or a wife so quickly. I wish I'd had
a chance to grow earlier. And then know where I was
going, rather than being sort of back to front like with
me. I sort of wonder how it would have been if. . . .'

CHAPTER 6

ARIADNE'S THREAD

One of the best known of the Greek myths is the story of Theseus and the Minotaur. Minos, the ruler of Crete, exacted a yearly tribute from Athens, in the form of seven youths and seven maidens to be devoured by the Minotaur, a monster with the head of a bull and the body of a man, which inhabited a labyrinth on the island. Theseus, son of the King of Athens, a young man who has already proved his courage by heroic deeds, sets sail for Crete as one of the sacrificial victims, intending to kill the monster. But the slaying of the Minotaur and Theseus' escape from the labyrinth are only achieved with the help of Ariadne, the Cretan king's daughter, who has fallen in love with Theseus. Ariadne gives him two things: a sword and a clue of thread by which to find his way out of the labyrinth. With the Minotaur slain, Theseus follows the thread and succeeds in escaping. With him he takes his fellow Athenians and Ariadne, though he is soon to abandon her on the island of Naxos. On his return to Athens he forgets to give the signal of his success, a white sail. Seeing the black sail in the horizon, Theseus' father kills himself in despair and Theseus himself becomes the king. One of his subsequent legendary exploits is to do battle against and defeat the Amazons. Having defeated them, he marries their queen, Hyppolita.

Although classical historians believe Theseus to have been a purely legendary person, he was glorified by the Athenian state at the height of its power as one of its early kings and credited with having been its true founder, through the unification of the scattered Attic communities. This historical recruitment of a mythical hero in the service of nationalism

– as an emblem of the state's strength, achievements and continuity – is only one among many examples of how legends have been elaborated to function as ideology. Over much longer periods of cultural consciousness their patterns of events and symbols have also come to function as lessons in human processes of development – Freud wrote of mythology as 'psychology projected into the external world', and saw the hero myth as the first, marking the advance from group psychology to individual psychology. It is not difficult to see in the Theseus stories a symbolic enactment of the male passage to maturity and the consolidation of male power.

The task that confronts Theseus is to kill a monster, but at the risk of his own life. Without Ariadne he would have no weapon, without her he would be unable to find his way back to safety and escape the wrath of King Kinos, her father. Ariadne is crucial to Theseus' success. With the (phallic) sword she has given him he can destroy the monster (and the power of his enemy) and with her thread he is guaranteed a safe return. He has triumphed over one patriarch, and by 'forgetting' his arrangement to warn his father of the outcome of his enterprise, unwittingly displaces him and himself assumes the central patriarchal power in Athens. By abandoning Ariadne he breaks the thread that builds him to her and affirms his independent power. With the later subjugation of the Amazon women he eliminates all female claims or threats.

Here is the quest for maturity and independence, as the young man takes the place of the old, and masculine continuities are maintained. Here is the denial of female ties and the validation of male dominance.

The Theseus legends exist in different versions and have evolved and been transformed into different kinds of stories in art and literature, so that there is room for a variety of allegorical interpretations. They pre-echo other familiar structures and progressions in the mythology of male heroes. The fictions of the western, the thriller or the detective story, and in particular the cinematic model of the *film noir*, all furnish some correspondences. In them the individual male proves himself by challenging another, more powerful, and usually older man. In the western this is done through the violent confrontation of the shoot-out, in the detective story/ thriller by unravelling the truth and unmasking the villain, with the narrative drive akin to the conquest of a labyrinth. And through the jagged chiaroscuro expressionism of the post-war *film noir*, heightened sex antagonisms – acute male paranoia and the threatening, often deadly, nature of the women – become pathologies of fear and desire.

These classic cycles of male heroism contain strong elements of resistance to ties with women, either because women as wives or sweethearts stand in the way of the freedoms without which the masculine code would collapse – individual moral fibre, endurance of physical hardships and pain (which are later rewarded with status): 'a man's gotta do . . .' – or because involvement with women is, because of their power, identified as a threat to male integrity and to masculinity itself, a threat which may have to be destroyed.

The equation between manhood and going it alone, needing nothing from women, has such mythic proportions that it pervades innumerable cultural expressions of masculinity. Men who would be better men if they freed themselves from women are stock characters in popular culture. At their crudest they are embodied in the working-class macho figures who inhabit cartoons and situation comedies, music-hall jokes and television commercials for beer. Self-sufficiency here is just straightforward misogyny, an assertion of a separate virile physicality defined through a manual labour. The idea of men as self-sufficient individuals held back by female hooks and claws dies hard, but male unemployment and the changing role of women have turned these into increasingly empty postures.

Ariadne's thread is a more accurate image for the ties that bind men to women: so fine that it is almost invisible, so necessary to man's survival that he cannot venture out to face the dangers of the world without it. He needs the security of knowing that he can find his way back – back to safety and the female nurturance that began with a mother.

Male dependency in adult relationships with women is an area of silence and sleights of hand, precisely because it is so threatening to men's social power. Men are supposed to protect women from danger, support them as breadwinners, and give them a rock-solid shoulder to cry on. Male vulnerability is a public taboo, any show of male weakness a social embarrassment and an erosion of status. The social prohibition of men's tears and fears is only lifted in the context of an intimate relationship. There men can reveal another side of themselves; they can be 'little boys', men having a respite from the rigours of manhood.

It's true that such self-surrender is a part of the popular romantic scenario, and it has also been implicit in a liberal softening of the male image that has occurred around the edges of middle-class life (particularly in the United States) over the last decade or so. In her book *The Hearts of Men*, Barbara Ehrenreich argues that an increasing number of men have repudiated the breadwinner role in the decades since the 1950s, with male rejection of traditional family responsibilities paralleling the progress of the women's movement, and with a re-writing of the masculine script prompted by such phenomena as the *Playboy* philosophy and the Beats, the 'growth' movement and gay liberation. But even with newly developed male sensitivities, men's expectations of women have, she concludes, changed little:

> As it is, male culture seems to have abandoned the breadwinner role without overcoming the sexist attitudes that role has perpetuated: on the one hand, the expectation of female nurturance and submissive service as a matter of right; on the other hand, a misogynist contempt for women as 'parasites' and entrappers of men.[1]

The realities of male dependency are obscured by men's

greater economic and social power. Men may find it a little easier to admit to vulnerability in private, but the *idea* that men are weaker than women in psychological terms has only a narrow social validation since it isn't borne out by their public lives.

As boys grew up taking it for granted that mother will provide for their practical domestic needs – cooking, laundry, mending and sundry details of everyday life – so that they will be free to get on with independent activities outside in the world, so men take it for granted that women will provide for their needs in the couple, and that women will also give them support and attention.

If this seems to describe only the most traditional pattern of couple relationships, in which the man is the breadwinner and the woman primarily a housewife, I'd suggest that it is always this pattern that sets some level of expectation in even those modern relationships where equality is a goal and where there is a commitment to share housework, to share childcare where there are children, and in a situation where incomes are equal and jobs equally important. This, of course, presupposes an equal starting base that only exists for a minority of couples, but it is worth considering how much such relationships are shadowed by earlier unequal models, if only to speculate on how much the internalised expectations and dynamics persist.

The pattern is set early in childhood for men to see home as a safe base from which to pursue their paths to freedom and independence in the world – with Ariadne's thread in hand to guide them back.

Women do have power over men. They have the power to meet their emotional needs by being open to their vulnerability, by guaranteeing all the safety of the domestic sphere and the continuity of the nurturance that the mother gave. It is a safety that men may take for granted once it is secured in a stable relationship, although this may be unacknowledged. What is hardest of all to acknowledge is their neediness and dependency. In an echo of the boy's later relationship to his mother he may disavow his dependence and assert his separateness and detatchment from the couple through work and other areas of his life outside it. It is not an unusual feature of this process for the man to perceive his independent impulses as being somehow thwarted or resisted by the woman (just as his mother might have behaved) even where this is not happening. This misapprehension may simply be an unconscious act of self-deceit whose outcome is to situate the women in a dependent and possessive relation to the man and reassure him of his greater power in the relationship. It is certainly easy for men to do this, allowing that they already have a strong sense of a socially and physically validated identity that exists independent of a domestic relationship, so that the containment of the couple can be experienced as claustrophobic. It is also easy to misrecognise the balance of dependency within a couple since men are less available to other people's emotional demands than women. While girls learn from an early age that it is their given role to nurture and care for others, and are expected to be 'emotional', boys are discouraged from displays of emotion and masculinity divorces itself from a concern with emotional life. In a relationship where a woman asks for as much emotional support and attention as she gives, she can soon appear to be making dependent demands. Yet the reality of the situation would be quite the contrary. The man may even be willing to give this support, but men often lack the vocabulary of emotional discourse or are ill at ease with it. Even just by *asking* for what the man cannot provide, the woman makes herself vulnerable to feelings of dependency. The paradox of the man's position is that by depending on a woman to an enormous degree he can appear to be independent.

Men have stronger boundaries, a sharper concentration on themselves to the exclusion of others, and they expect others to respect these boundaries. 'Don't disturb Daddy, he's working. . . .'

Why do I find it so hard to resist M's interruptions while I'm working: chats, cups of tea, questions? If I interrupt him

*when he's absorbed in a piece of work I am warned off. I
sometimes remind him that he doesn't think twice about
cutting in on my concentration. He remembers and takes
heed – for a day or two.*

Men have access to better defences than women when it is
necessary to camouflage their vulnerability. Men who lack
confidence can disguise this by a display of masculine attitudes. I have known men who were opinionated and bossy,
who adopted a superior manner towards women and
appeared powerful as a result, yet gradually it was possible to
see through this demeanour to severe feelings of inadequacy.
Feminist women, seen as powerful by such men, are liable to
fill them with anxiety. Male bluster and arrogance may make
it hard to recognise the weakness that it conceals precisely
because we don't expect weakness from men.

Yet women are well aware of men's vulnerability. But at
one remove from their own. It tends to take them by surprise
when it breaks the surface of male containment, betraying
real, desperate fears of loss. It is so much of a shock that
women are sometimes overwhelmed by its intensity, by its
acknowledgment of their own power, so much so that they
feel responsible and guilty, and will hasten to reassure, to
restore the male equilibrium that previously existed, and
allow men to resume control. Joanna Watt described her
conflicting emotions in the face of her boyfriend's deception
about an affair he was having with someone else:

'I went to stay with a friend that night. He insisted on
driving me round there, then did this whole crumbling
act in the car, by the end of which I felt guilty and as if
I'd been horrible. It's all the things about being a woman
and being sympathetic and being understanding and
comforting . . . I also did manage to keep the absolute
fury, and yet somehow that just gets dissipated by this
little boy act: "I can't cope without you" sort of thing.'

She perceives Jim's 'crumbling' as a controlling kind of behaviour: 'it was still in a power-trip way.'

But why are women so susceptible to such displays of male emotion? Why is it so easy to experience them as overwhelming, even paralysing, as undermining the very power they appear to bestow?

Not all men are so controlling as Jim. Joanna compares him with Jeff whom she lived with a few years before and observes that although he was less conscious of sexism 'he was naturally more egalitarian. He didn't have such an ego as Jim's got.' (With Jim, the sexual politics are a high-profile feature of the relationship; it's the powerful personality that Joanna has to contend with.) Yet even with men who appear to have a much smaller investment in a macho identity than Jim, women can find themselves caught in the same dynamic.

It is hard not to feel your own control being swept away by a tide of male guilt after confronting a man with feelings of hurt or anger, or with a demand for a decision. To women who have occupied the 'other women' role in a triangle this must be painfully familiar. The scenario is a common one: a man who is married or living with one woman falls in love with another. The affair becomes all the more passionate and exciting by virtue of its forbidden aspects, its sense of freedom from the constraints of routine domesticity and everyday responsibilities. It is a situation whose inequalities are compounded by the past: for the woman by the resonance of the family triangle in which the woman relives herself as the child in relation to mother and father – and for the man by the memory association of leaving the security of the maternal home for the unknown, uncertain of whether he can be sure of finding it elsewhere.

In this triangle the man holds the power; yet the classic circumstance is one where he is indecisive, unable to choose, to give up one woman for another, even where he perceives the first relationship to be unfulfilling. Men often delay this step for years. Some women wait patiently, until the ties that bind him to the first relationship have worn so thin that the thread snaps. Sometimes the stalemate is broken by the wife's decision to tolerate it no longer and leave the man who hasn't had the courage to leave her. But where the 'other woman' reaches the point when she decides to insist on commitment or an end to the relationship, it forces out some of the deep contradictions in the nature of male power within sexual relationships. For men find it hard to face up to responsibility for their emotions. Their intimate relationships with women are founded on an emotional dependency that is largely unacknowledged and disavowed – and much of the time projected on to the woman. When these emotions and the reality of this dependency are yanked into the open by the crisis of choice, a common male response is to abdicate responsibility. An inability to choose, an inability to help himself, an accession of guilt.

Not just in this, the situation of the emotional triangle, but in many aspects of relationships with men, women must carry the weight of emotional responsibilities and the burden of male dependency in this respect.

What this means for women is that they are better equipped to survive without the close support of a sexual love relationship than men. Even though it is harder for women socially to be partnerless, in the most personal and private areas of their lives it is probably more difficult for men to cope without a partner than it is for a woman. Women can draw on well-developed emotional resources and emotional closeness to women friends to combat loneliness. The prescriptions of masculinity mean that men lack these things or only possess them in small measure.

But what male dependency also means is a barrier to women's full sense of having control of their lives. It means a struggle within relationships to take equal responsibility and to hold on to emotional space. For a woman who is not in a relationship it means a fear that a man will make so many claims on her that her sense of a separate identity will be threatened.

Much is changing in the landscape of relationships between

men and women. The changes evolve in fine detail as well as
in the wider picture. The confidence women acquire in the
world outside – at work, in trade unions, in women's groups
and adult education classes – is brought into the domestic
reckoning. In mining communities all over Britain the wives
and girlfriends, mothers and sisters of men who weathered
the strike for over a year are reaping some of the benefits – as
well as the bitterness – of that experience. Women organised
throughout the strike, as women, but not just as back-up
sandwich makers and soup ladlers in the community kitchen.
They took a more prominent role than in past strike organisation, and carried their voices out to where they could be
heard at meetings and rallies, in print and on television
screens, to express the women's experience. For the first time
many took their place on miners' picket lines, and many for
the first time felt the exhilaration of having a central position
in political organisation. The lessons of the strike, and of
how public politics intersect with personal experience, are
still being learned in miners' kitchens and living rooms and
are being carried over into the atmosphere of daily life and
the balance of responsibility in families and relationships.

In May 1984, at the first demonstration of Women Against
Pit Closures, in Barnsley, Yorkshire, Lorraine Bowler told
10,000 women from mining areas all over Britain:

> 'Organisation has always been seen as an area belonging
> to men. We are seen to be the domestic element of a
> family. This for too many years has been the role expected
> of us. I have seen change coming for years and the last
> few years have seen it at its best.'

Julie Menéndez remarks earlier in this book that while she
has had periods of being alone and without a sexual relationship, the man she had separated from ten years earlier had
never been without a woman in his life in all that time. Men
need a woman in their lives perhaps a good deal more than
a woman needs a man: their independence depends upon it.

But more and more women are fighting for relationships that are on their terms as well as their partner's, and as a result more men are being compelled to engage with their demands, and to recongise their own dependency for what it is. The flight from emotional responsibility may well be turned back if Ariadne no longer holds the thread.

CHAPTER 7

MOTHERHOOD ... TO HAVE OR HAVE NOT?

Anybody can be a mother. An oyster can be a mother. The difficult thing is to be a person. *Charlotte Perkins Gilman*

I think a woman should be on her guard against the trap of motherhood and marriage. Even if she would dearly like to have children, she ought to think seriously about the conditions under which she would have to bring them up, because being a mother these days is real slavery. Fathers and society leave sole responsibility for the children to the mother. Women give up their jobs to look after small children. Women stay at home when the child has measles. And women are blamed if the child doesn't succeed.

If a woman still wants a child in spite of everything, it would be better to have one without getting married, because marriage is really the biggest trap of all.

... I'm not against mothers, but the ideology which expects every woman to have children ... *Simone de Beauvoir, 1976*[1]

'I had no idea what the responsibility would mean. I feel really grown-up for the first time in my life. When you have a child your life can't revolve around yourself.' *34-year-old single mother, 1985.*

At a friend's afternoon birthday party, as adults and children mill around, it suddenly dawns on me that I'm the only woman there who isn't a mother. It feels like a moment of truth to realise that I belong to a diminishing minority. The flurry of parental introductions (this is Tom's mum . . . Susie's dad . . . Andrew's little girl . . .) doesn't last, and new guests whom I can, with relief, recognise as fellow non-parents trickle in. But it's hard to banish this picture of myself as not only different, but defective – lacking in a common attribute. Perhaps I've consciously ignored the fact that most people of my generation have children, even those for whom the attractions of parenthood had never featured just a few years ago. I am perplexed that so many women have made this choice.

'Children are mainly ignored and kept separate in our society. I wanted people to bring their kids and not have to worry about babysitting' explained the friend later, when I confessed how I'd felt. 'You probably wouldn't have felt like that if you were more used to children being around; if they were more accepted, the way they are in Latin countries.'

I wonder. In most societies children are largely an individual responsibility. Having them and looking after them is up to parents, with varying degrees of state and municipal intervention, often no more than a minimal commitment to nursery education. They involve parental decisions, parental problems; yet, since children are our connection to the future they are, or should be, a social responsibility. How far can individual choices and social responsibility be reconciled? I think about planned economies, the Chinese government's ban on more than one child per couple. No solutions there. Collectivised childcare and the breaking down of traditional divisions between wage labour and domestic labour are still feminist ideals, but when I look at the feminist mothers I know, most are enclosed in narrow family units: two parents or just a mother and child, coping single-handed with work and the demands of childcare, with only informal networks of friends to help out at half past three when school or nursery comes out, or when children are in bed with one of the many ailments and illnesses that punctuate early childhood.

When I've watched other women struggle with the strain of sleepless nights and crying babies, often as mothers for the first time in their thirties, even forties, after years of autonomy, I am appalled by the difficulties of it, the enormous loss of freedom, the financial pressures as income shrinks. I wonder why they do it. Why do women today decide to have children?

This may seem a presumptuous question in a world which has never ceased to reproduce, in a world where the majority of adults beyond a certain age appear to be parents, in a world where people will go to enormous lengths to bring a child into their lives – through adoption or *in vitro* fertilisation – even if biology denies them one. Having children is an unquestionable fact of life.

There are good reasons for having children: they are funny, beautiful, entertaining, a source of many joys and delights. There are also good reasons for not having them – besides the fact that they can also be a source of worry and anxiety. They are, as Simone de Beauvoir says, a trap for women. Women's responsibility for children repeatedly frustrates their aspiration for fulfilment in other areas of their lives. It confirms women in a role that has oppressively defined them for centuries.

Why, then, should so many women who have aspired to independence and been the active agents of so many changes affecting women's status, who have access to free contraception and legal abortion, who have in many ways shaped new answers to the question of what it is to be a woman – why should so many of them continue to choose motherhood, despite its propensity to stun and shackle and bring their utopian dreams bumpily down to earth? Why the feminist rush to maternity?

Contradiction. Of couse. The desire to have everything, to miss out on no experience, to cram everything into one life. We all have that. But shouldn't rationality prevail when it's evident that there's a price to be paid? Do they all suffer from an irresistible biological urge unknown only to me and a handful of other childless sympathisers? Or is it social pressure; the domino effect as one enlarged tummy after another prompts thoughts of baby bliss and you feel you have to join the club? Or is it to give a meaning to life when all else seems to have failed?

A mother humours me: 'I think a lot of people do get broody; they have a physical strong urge for babies. Then there are others who don't have that at all, but they panic when the biological time-clock starts ticking away fast, so they get pregnant without thinking about the future. Maybe it happens by accident and you realise that this is your last chance; if you have an abortion it becomes final and that's too hard to handle.'

Then there's the desire to close the space of the couple in a circle of three; the ultimate fulfilment of a relationship, love made flesh.

Given that we can't have everything, whatever decision we make is muddied with ambivalence. Motherhood is a choice all women face (even infertility, which women often only discover after planning a pregnancy, imposes renewed choice over courses of action). If we choose not to have children, that decision may remain with us as the ghost of something we might have had, but lost. At the root of our feelings there may be curiosity, sentiment, the knowledge of forfeiting a vital and important experience, the urge to invest the future in another human being, or sundry hidden impulses. Some women live with a measure of regret in their choice; some scarcely notice they've made it.

I have never particularly wanted to have children. I don't now, although I wonder what it would have been like, and think sometimes that I am cutting myself off from the future.

Even as I write I feel on the defensive, compelled to justify what must seem an unnatural attitude. I feel the compulsion to do so comes not just from the world out there, where the equation of womanhood and femininity with motherhood is writ large, but also from other feminist women. Every woman who acts on her desire to have a child has to turn her back on what it would have meant to have made the other choice. Does she forget what that would have meant? Can she imagine that her desire for motherhood may be quite unknown to other women?

Women who choose not to become mothers, either because they are unattracted by the prospect or because they feel there is too high a price to pay, also want to feel that their decision is respected as their right. They want to be supported in that choice. Mothers want to be supported in theirs, both in the rightness of the decision, and in the practical and psychological realities of motherhood. Here there is a tension.

It is an inevitable tension. Having a child changes your life – if you are a woman; less so if you are a man. The women's movement has been caught between the need to affirm the significance of women's experience as bearers and carers of children and the value of the practical and emotional work involved, and the need to argue for men to take an equal share in responsibility for children. Some strands of feminism have emphasised the first to the exclusion of the second, while many who are convinced that the second is an essential goal still find themselves trapped inside the frustrations of a role that demands enormous amounts of energy, time and self-effacement but whose significance is still overlooked. Women are pursued by guilt and anxiety about whether they are good enough as mothers, even when reason tells them that the burden of responsibility is being unequally divided.

To dissolve some of this tension it is necessary to think of how things might be different, to envisage scenarios where the choice is not so drastic and where parenthood is not a burden for individual women, not a set of socially prescribed duties that exclude other possibilities.

In a recent article on motherhood and utopias,[2] Sheila Rowbotham compared two contrasting feminist fictions: *Herland*, written by Charlotte Perkins Gilman in 1915, and Marge Piercy's *Woman on the Edge of Time*, written in 1976. *Herland*, with all the didacticism of a tract intended for male edification, describes women's capabilities and their potential to thrive without men, in a country where no men exist and where the supreme values – those of mothering – are elevated to the status of a religion. *Woman on the Edge of Time* is a fantasy in which a woman in a repressive mental institution travels through time to discover a happier future society organised in democratic, small-community units in which relationships are free of sexual jealousy and emotional inhibitions. It is also a world which is ecologically conscious and socially androgynous; women's equality has finally been achieved by the elimination of maternal biology – children are bred in machines, every child has three carers and all equally nurture and nurse, since men have even developed the capacity to breastfeed.

As Sheila Rowbotham observes, *Herland* is hardly a liberating utopia for women who have no desire to be mothers or to see mothering as a central and dominant aspect of their lives. Like her, I have more enthusiasm for Marge Piercy's vision, although, as she also remarks, 'It seems profoundly pessimistic to assume there cannot be equality while this difference remains between men and women.'

Such technological possibilities are no longer unthinkable, but to eliminate that difference in ways that will benefit women, rather than merely take from them what one of Marge Piercy's characters calls 'the only power we ever had', presupposes enormous changes on many fronts. Meanwhile, the best that can be done is to inch towards them by making childcare and other forms of domestic labour integral demands in any strategy for social and economic change. It's an economic model that's hard to imagine at present.[3] But the last decade has seen a proliferation of support systems for women's demands for a transformation of childcare responsibilities and reproductive control. As one mother said, 'The National Childbirth Trust has grown so much and has so much support that there's nothing strange or women's libby in complaining about maternity services these days.' Older campaigns and associations have been consolidated in the last few years, and new ones have sprung up. A worker for the London Childcare Network, founded in 1984 and linking projects and nurseries all over the city, told me that she was convinced that its momentum would continue, despite the cuts in public money for childcare provision.

On the home front there are isolated but significant signs of the desire to transform traditional divisions of childcare responsibility. One mother, a full-time polytechnic lecturer with a 3-year-old looked after by a childminder, has resisted giving up part of her job and, instead, her partner, also a lecturer, has cut his work down to a four-day week so that he can spend more time with his son. Another mother, a free-lance film-maker, works full-time and often travels abroad while her husband takes on the role of primary parent to their 10-year-old, does the housework and cooking and takes care of her accounts – in a complete role reversal. A group of six – two single parents and two sets of married parents – have a formal childcare network for their under-5s. All of these are just people I happen to know. They also happen to have relatively well-paid jobs. Such deviations from conventional patterns may seem like simply a luxury for well-placed parents with money or mobility, but are also something of a necessity if ideas are to shift, even in small ways. Their inadequacies as limited lifestyle changes are apparent in the case of one mother who, after being involved in setting up and running a full-time neighbourhood creche with friends, found her circumstances hugely altered when she followed her child's father in a move to another city and became locked into the syndrome of the isolated housewife and mother.

If we do choose to have children, the reckoning, in terms of what we gain, and what we risk losing, is incalculable. The realities of motherhood vary enormously. Even among that portion of women in western society who have been directly touched by the women's movement there is a great variety of experience, attitudes and theories about mothering and childcare.

The key word here *is* choice. The fact that we can now

be sexual women without our sexuality being tethered to reproduction has meant the growth of our potential to assert our independence from biology. My own generation (I was born in 1947) was the first to take that for granted.

Although I know that motherhood would give my life an entirely new dimension, it is impossible for me to contemplate the emotional and practical consequences without being convinced of loss. Yet the choice *not* to have children is rarely respected as valid in itself. Given a conventional set of circumstances – like a stable couple and secure housing – it's often seen as perverse. It's assumed that all women *want* to have children. The dominance of this assumption is underestimated. While mothers have to have more recognition and the world has to be reorganised to account for the needs of children and parents, there has to be an equal acceptance of the option not to have children. As it is, parenthood is a cultural inevitability; it comes hard to many women to view it as a matter of choice. 'I think the National Childcare Campaign should be actively campaigning on behalf of women who do not want to have children, and that that is something of status in our society,' argued one of the Campaign's long-standing activists in a recent interview – a comment I found heartening and at the same time startling for its acknowledgment that while mothers are undervalued, woman who refuse motherhood pay other social penalties, or, perhaps more accurately, the vague threat of being marginal and different is what weighs the balance of self-image. Being a mother is a source of definable identity and creative satisfactions, particularly if the possibilities for such satisfactions are limited elsewhere in life. Being a *mother* still means more than being a *parent*.

Choices about motherhood and how women live its realities are influenced by many things, not least by our own experience as daughters. Women are often conscious of repeating some of the patterns they saw in their mothers, but are also capable of breaking them and reshaping them with the possibilities of their own lives and a different time. They are often all too aware of their own mothers' contradictions and resentments about mothering. They want to avoid passing these on to their children, but it's sometimes necessary to acknowledge the difficulty of transcending emotions grounded in the continuous character of a relationship, and in the history of motherhood as self-sacrifice.

For me motherhood would be incompatible with what I regard as a necessary independence. It would involve the loss of too much. I think women are owed more support and esteem as parents, and, like Simone de Beauvoir, I'm not against mothers. But I'm truly grateful for her rejection of the ideology which expects every woman to have children.

Joanna Watt and Claire Booth are both feminists. Both have young children. But in most other respects they are very different: in their background, their living situations, and their feelings about motherhood. Joanna lives with her child's father, Claire lives alone with her children. Joanna expresses a need to resist being absorbed into the identity 'mother'; Claire feels that she only truly achieved a feminine identity when she gave birth, and delights in being seen as a mother. Joanna feels that she couldn't have had a child alone, facing single parenthood; Claire finds it less complicated to bring up her children without a man around.

But Joanna and Claire do not represent antagonistic points of view, neither are they typical of one kind of feminist attitude or another. Their different emotions and different strategies for dealing with the pressures on women as mothers suggest just how complex these are, and they give us clues to the deeper sources of women's dilemmas as mothers.

Joan Rodney's account of her life follows the accounts of Claire and Joanna. It opens quite another perspective on the question of motherhood and independence. It was only through the decision to have a first child in her forties that Joan's life could take a new direction, from a job in a factory to higher education. Her experience reminds us of how many kinds of change are needed before choice is a real freedom for women.

CLAIRE BOOTH 'If you've got small children, it's very hard to go out and be with other people and socialise. Friends sometimes come, and you want to be with them, but because you're pretty tired anyhow, there are limits to how much you can lead a life as though the children didn't exist. And another hard thing is that physically it's just extremely hard work. You've got to be up at seven every day of the year – unless I've got my mother here, or somebody who'll say, "Stay in bed and I'll get them up for you." And even then you don't feel quite free. The best sleep I've ever had in all this time was one time when I'd sent them round to somebody else, and I thought well I'm bound to wake up at 8 o'clock in the morning, and I slept till 10. And just because they weren't there. I was on my own – and somebody that afternoon said, "You look so well, have you been on holiday?" It was just a good night's sleep. Otherwise, there's never anybody to do those things, whether they're ill or you're ill or whatever happens. Even though I have a lot of help, people without children, people with children.

'I don't resent them at all. Sometimes I . . . sometimes I just wish they weren't there, I wish I didn't have to wake up at seven, I wish I didn't have to get up, I wish somehow they would be active and secure and I would go on sleeping. But I don't feel any resentment against them. I do think it's a very big strain, because any time that you're tired, and they're demanding at that precise moment more and more, you have to take a very firm and artificial grip on yourself and, and . . . keep calm, or whatever. I'm aware that sometimes if I'm around I'm withdrawing from them, if I feel too tired and they're wanting a story or they're wanting to play and so forth, I'm just constantly saying, "Yes I'm just coming," and really I'm hoping that the more I say that the more they'll just find something else and get on with it on their own. I've read about this withdrawing recently and I realise I do a fair amount of that, I just find other busy things to do, to involve me . . . I mean partly I feel you can't be constantly entertaining children, they jolly well have to find their own way, partly you just don't feel like it. I'm not the sort of person who particularly likes playing childish games anyhow. Really it's a bore playing snap with children, it's a boring game and they have to win all the time. It's fun seeing how delighted they are to win, but I find every excuse in the book not to play snap.

'I have the morning space, and I have a sort of panicky awareness with my eye on the clock all the time, that I've got to do various things, then get back and pick them up. So I'm desperately trying to do as much as I can in that time. And I have an evening space, which is also circumscribed. But then if I just sit down and watch telly or whatever, never mind how late it ends and how nice it's going to be, that's real relaxation. . . . I still am constantly nagged if I do anything after eleven p.m. then I pay for it the next morning, and particularly it might be a morning when they wake up at six or half past. . . . I think personally anyhow I find it very difficult to sit down and do nothing. And I've got every excuse to tell myself I can't possibly do that, because there's a list as long as my arm of things I've got to be getting on with and doing. But I don't think it's entirely because of them, and I don't think *any* of these things are entirely because of them. I think it's partly with me as a person. I've been doing this for years, finding it very difficult to have time off, and I'm not sure that the tiredness is altogether because of them. I think the tiredness is also partly because of – if I actually went to bed later, but I was doing so because I was out having a good time with somebody, I think I wouldn't feel so tired necessarily; it's partly the tiredness that's the constant feeding out of emotion. . . . I get tremendous emotions straight back from them, but they're infantile ones, you know they're not the sort of adult support you'd get in a relationship or something, and that's not being fed back into me. I think that's partly the sole burden in itself, then a trap you get into because you say you haven't got time, it's late, and so on and so forth. You must get out, it's true enough, but you can't get out because you're tired, but you're tired partly because you *don't* get out. All the same, there's just no denying that bringing up small children on your own is physically very tiring.

'I used to go once a week to this job, and I now only go sort of irregularly . . . it was a much longer break in the morning than I have. It wasn't really the number of hours that I worked there, but the fact that it was a completely different world in which I was not just with babies but I actually was involved in and doing things with adults. It was extremely hard work. . . . And I think that developing my social life wouldn't be a question of how many parties I went to, but I would actually be involved in something outside home that was equally absorbing, and obviously, that also involves being involved with a man that would emotionally be deeply absorbing with him and the children. That would be a great big plus. And I don't know how to engineer that.

'A lot of people can't go out because they can't afford to pay somebody to look after their children. And, at the very basic level, money for domestic appliances – if you haven't got a washing machine, or even haven't got a washing up machine – why not? Because people spend hours washing up every day. I think money's very important. And a good relationship with somebody who actually persuades a mother to take time for herself, to allow time for herself. And I don't think it's just me, I think it's very, very difficult to do . . . guilt I suppose.

'It's very difficult to put children into nursery full-time I think, not that there's a lot of them available. If they were available you might give yourself a lot more anguish about whether it was the right thing for them, whether they're happy there, or you were saying goodbye to them before they'd started. When the children were very young I had people living in to help, and that was fantastic, because they were at home but I didn't need to look after them all the time. I know they'd be perfectly happy in a nursery. But it's quite difficult, unless you start it very young, to break yourself. . . . And for my sake too. I mean I feel I'm going to lose them so soon. I don't mind losing them bit by bit. But if I'd had to go back to work when they were 6 or 10 months old and I'd been in a full-time job, I would have worried for *them*, but I would have been terribly broken-hearted *myself*. Feeling I was missing them. I think I'm very dependent on them, but that's a vicious circle really, because if you don't have other emotional focuses in your life, then they become a very important one. And that's self-justifying in a way, because they are obviously still very young, and they've only got one parent, I think that's a problem for them before you start. If they're then going to leave that one parent quite a lot of the time, even though it would be a regular, stable substitute, that substitute might only be for six months or a year at a time, and it's quite a big thing to embark on. In no way am I saying that people who leave their children in a nursery are doing the wrong thing. Apart from anything else, I can't see any bad effects on the children who are. Just that I would find it very hard and very painful. . . . To me they're the most joyful, beautiful, wonderful creatures – although ghastly some of the time – but they are. And also, the quality of love is so – despite everything – is so sort of unconditional, and they're so fascinating, that I don't want to give them up!

'And in a way that gets stronger, or very very strong.

They're very much into verbal affection now. They tell
you how much they love you, and you tell them how
much you love *them*. And really it's a love-making, and
in which the whole reality of oedipal triangles and
fixations and so on becomes absolutely real. It's a very
powerful thing. Nonetheless, I know people who have
gone back to work, who've found it, certainly at the
time, very painful, and then have settled down perfectly
happily and still have the same qualities and in a sense
have a richness in their lives from having their children
and from having the other parts of their lives. Whether
other single parents find that I'm not sure, but it's precisely
the single parents who often *do* have to go back to work,
who do have to put their children in the nursery.

'I know there's all this evidence about the quality of
relationships and time spent between children and
parents, rather than the quantity – that it's much better
to have a few hours of face-to-face and playing and so
on, rather than endless days of frustration and shut-inness
and boredom and being at loggerheads all the time. So
there's nothing categorical to be said about it, when it
comes to talking about my dependence on them and my
particular situation.

'You've got a whole identity, a maternal identity. If you
were married or with somebody you could almost not
even bother about your whole status as a sort of sexually
feminine woman any more, because you're a mother. If
you're not, and you're hoping you're going to meet
somebody, then you've got to haul in the whole business
of getting yourself together as a woman in order to find
somebody, as well as just muddling along as a mother.
I think I know exactly why women don't bother with new
clothes, fashion etcetera any more, once they've got
children. I suppose they might be scared of losing their
husbands, but they've got an ultra-feminine identity. I
don't think all women feel this, but for me being feminine
meant having children – perhaps I always found other
kinds of femininity very difficult to accomplish. I never

felt I was quite right as a woman, but I'm terribly proud,
I'm slightly embarrassed to admit, but I'm terribly proud
of telling people I've got children, and being a mother,
and walking round with them holding their hands, and I
think the worst thing that could have happened to me
in my life is that I would never had had children. It would
have been the most dreadful blow to my sense of myself.

Support

'When the children were little and I didn't have a car, I
was much more mobile than most people are, I mean I
had to put them both in the buggy, go on the train, on
the tube, it was hard enough on buses. I did get around
a lot. I think I was actually determined to get around. If
I wanted to go and see my sister on the other side of
London then I'd just have to get there. I did. It was a
terrific strain, and very hard work going down the
escalators and so on. And having a car just means that if
they're getting really difficult and bad moods and so on
you can just drop everything and go off. Otherwise your
whole geography is much more limited.

'I think that space, a large flat, has made a lot of
difference. It would be a lot harder to be cooped up with
them in a small space, as women often are. For me now
the ideal with small children would be a small bungalow
with a garden all round. . . . I have a family in the country,
and a family at all is absolutely crucial, a family fairly
nearby. I'm very well off. And although I have to work
a bit hard for my money, no financial practical worries
at all. Even if I ran out, I know somebody would be there.
I mean I lurch along, a lot of the time, I haven't got any
doom feelings at all.

'I do think a crucial difference is having been in the
women's movement, and having friends from the
women's movement, with whom I don't just have a social
exchange and ordinary chitchat. I mean I have a lot of
friends now who are good, who I have a lot in common
with because we have children the same age, but there's

very few of them that I can call on; in terms of practical crisis they could help me out, but it would be difficult to call on them in terms of emotional crisis. Not because they wouldn't be nice and helpful, but it's not a mutual thing at all – they wouldn't call on me, partly because they're with a man, but not necessarily. Whereas the women's movement, those are people I have a long history with – as a matter of course one's talked all sorts of emotional things, and even if they don't have children or know anything about the experience of children at all. If it had been twenty years ago I wouldn't have had that. We've read about it, talked to each other about it, recognised it as a political thing rather than personal shortcomings.

'I mean I just couldn't contemplate having children on my own even with the women's movement. When Peter and I decided to break up I was actually horrified – I just couldn't think I'd manage at all. I used to think were I to have children on my own I just couldn't face it. I thought it was just a different kind of person, a stronger person. Fine for them, but not for me. I didn't think I was strong enough to do that. I mean I'm a very self-reliant person, but self-reliant people give themselves an awful lot of trouble. I sometimes wish I was more dependent. As a self-reliant person you turn more and more and more into yourself rather than simply not being able to take it and somehow ending up with someone who'll look after you. Only I long for someone to look after me. I think it's inevitable. I am very self-reliant and I *seem* exceedingly self-reliant and competent, maybe sometimes putting too much strain on myself.'

JOANNA WATT 'Motherhood has made me feel that I cannot take for granted space and time that I had before. Like tonight I just came in feeling that I could not go on. I was just so haggard that all I could do was retreat on to the sofa and be a child myself. Instead of which I've got her making demands on me. Obviously that's a profound change, that you always are conscious of this needy individual. And the other thing is always having to plan time. You can't do things spontaneously, unless I know that Jim's going to be at home. There's that whole dimension of planning your life. It's a whole thing about your psychology as well. Like now I'm going to start a new job. I don't feel terribly able to go into it just thinking what am I going to be doing? All the time it's mediated by Janie, and I've got to be able to be at home at certain times and certain days. I've found that quite difficult I suppose. Although at the same time because I'm a lot more tired than I would have been, in some ways I'm more ready to spend the time at home. I spend a lot more time at home than I ever did before.

'But I've got the most freedom that is possible if you've got a child. However rough my job's been for the last period I've still never felt tempted to give it up, even though I suppose I couldn't afford to, anyway. But I suppose I could afford to go part-time or something. I don't want to. It would actually drive me mad to be stuck in the house all day. Ideally I would in some ways like to work part-time. You see the problem is not work and Janie, it's trying to do other things as well. It would be manageable if you just had work and a child, but when you're also trying to be politically active and other things, it's all too much.

'Because you're a mother you're expected to have contact with other mothers, even when you've got bugger all in common apart from the fact that you've both got offspring 6 months old to 18 months. So when I've been the odd time to the baby club, OK it's been all right as a one-off thing, but I really couldn't bear that . . . it's absolutely boring; people just talk about babies. I think the other reason why I wouldn't work part-time is because I think we are validated a lot through our work, through the fact that we have *real jobs* as it were. I think that still part-time jobs are not regarded as real work. If I gave up my full-time job I think I'd be worried that I'd be seen as a "housewife and mother really", and just doing a bit of a job. Because they did ask me at this new job if I wanted to job-share, and I said no. It's so insecure as well. If I did part-time teaching work I would lose all my security, as well as status. And money. You can't do a part-time scale 3 job, you can only do a part-time scale 1 job.

'That's one thing I have felt very strongly, that I want to be economically independent. That's really important to me. I think probably sometimes too much.

'Being supported by a man would be tempered by all those things that I've talked about already: housework, childcare, other people's perceptions of how you should be. At least now I feel at the end of the day I can turn round and say I work full-time, therefore it's not Jim being good when he does these things, it's actually because we both have full-time jobs and we need to share the other things too. Whereas that would actually be much more difficult to argue with people outside feminism. And also, what I find when I work at home is that the bloody stuff does encroach on me – like when I was on maternity leave, and I was off from July through all of September and I started doing part-time tuition work. I was supposed to be studying for a diploma I'd started and I found it difficult, because I noticed that something needed doing or I felt obliged to cook the meal or whatever. And you can just stay at home and fill up your time, even though you know that you're supposed to be beyond that. I mean it sort of takes you back to the Feminine Mystique.

'The thing I always know at the end of the day is that if we split up I could still economically survive without Jim. That's really important – to have that sort of security, however painful and hurtful it might be. At the level of gritty reality, then I could manage quite easily. With me that's always underlying the situation, which I regard as a privileged position compared with most women. Women like Jim's mum and his sister-in-law who do the childcare for Janie while we're at work.

The original arrangement was that Jim's mum would do it, but then when his brother was made redundant Shirley thought they could do with the money so the two of them share it. I think that's cushioned a lot for us. I mean it would – there was no chance of a nursery place, no way I was going to get one. The only one that possibly I may get would only be until 4.40, so it's not terribly useful if you've got to work longer hours.

'They wouldn't be able to do it if we weren't in a position to pay them properly. Shirley badly needs the money. Jim's mum might have done, I suppose, just because she wouldn't like to think I'd hive Janie off to any minder I could get. But she actually finds it very difficult not to have any money. She was working in a launderette, doing service washes, and she gave it up except for a few hours a week and looked after Janie the rest of the time. In fact now she would not have been working at all, because the launderette closed.

'As a result of her doing childcare I think I've got a much closer relationship with her than I would have had. But it's funny; even though I go out to work just like Jim, and she looks after Janie, she still addresses all the domestic things to me.

'That's hard for me – although I sort of say things and often she'll say, "Oh, I didn't mean to say that," but I think it still comes back at some point in your head, however much you think you've got it sorted out, there's still a level of guilt about it. You know, you're not being a proper mother or proper woman in the home. And that is the crucial difference. I experience pressure and guilt as a result of other people – whereas Jim couldn't

give a damn what other people think. He wouldn't feel
at all put out if things were an absolute shambles,
whereas I would feel responsible.

'The other thing is that if men do anywhere near half
the domestic things, they're seen as being good. With
having Janie I've had more contact with women round
here who I wouldn't otherwise have had anything to do
with – outside feminist circles. There's this woman who
comes round who's got quite a small child. She's got
quite close to Jim's mum, so she comes popping in – and
I've got nothing in common with her, absolutely nothing,
apart from the fact that we've both got infants. She's got
this absolute shit of a husband; she never knows when
he's coming in, but his tea's still got to be done. She has
literally not had any time off since she had the baby,
about nine months ago, just none. And yet she makes me
feel that I should somehow be grateful for the fact that
– she doesn't say it directly, but it's there – that Jim is
good. And I don't think he is at all.

'The other thing that's difficult is to get away from
Janie. I've only had a weekend totally on my own, and
then days, if Jim's had a conference and taken her to a
creche, or if I've gone out for the day. I can remember
when she was very tiny just being really exhilarated by
going to a conference once, just because I'd been cooped
up – that's how it felt. Something I would have before
taken as just a matter of course, really felt like this great
event. When she was about ten days old I went out for
the day and left her with friends, and that felt really an
important thing to do.

'I think what surprises me is how much women tie
themselves to kids. Obviously there's a whole load of
things you can't do very much about; you are tied. But
at the same time, like for example breastfeeding, one
feels quite ambivalent. So many women I've known seem
to have tied themselves to the child because they weren't
prepared to offer the child anything other than the breast.

I remember going out for the day with this woman who had had her baby on the same day as me. The whole time we were out it was a total preoccupation. She wasn't separate from the child at all, she was totally obsessed with the fact that she was producing milk, how was the baby going to feel when it was left.

'Sometimes I feel worried because Celia, this other friend who's got a child, well her child's much more into her. As soon as Celia arrives everything else ceases and the child rushes to her. Whereas when I come home, Janie might smile or acknowledge the fact that I've come in, but it's certainly no big deal. And then sometimes I think, well sometimes I feel I'm not a proper mother. She's going through a phase at the moment where she's much more conscious of separation from Jim than she is of me.

'Sometimes if I'm sitting doing a typical maternal thing, which isn't very often actually – I play with her, but I don't sort of sit down and cuddle her in that baby position – at moments when I do sit like that there are times when I get a lot of pleasure from it. But really a lot of the time if I'm tired, what I worry about is that I'm not motherly enough. I just feel very conscious that I've got needs too and that she's got to learn that she isn't the only person in the universe.

'The biggest thing really, and a thing I get quite resentful about – and then I feel annoyed with myself because I feel I shouldn't get resentful – is just time being a luxury. I mean not doing anything much apart from being with Janie, I feel in some ways the pleasure goes out of your life. That Saturday night when you'd have gone out before, suddenly becomes this precious time when you can actually sit down. Studying has been important to me and still is, but I find I get less and less time to do it, and as a result I find myself in this position where time is so precious that I don't want to do so-called pleasurable things. But the biggest difficulty is just trying to concentrate when I'm tired. It was easier when she was smaller, because she would go to sleep for three hours and you'd get on and do something. I think that's another interesting contrast between me and Jim: if I'm with Jamie and she's awake, I find it almost impossible to sit and read or do something else, whereas quite often if he's got Janie during the day then he'll have some work in his hand at the same time. In other contexts I'm able to be quite relentless if I'm working, but it's just that I find it *impossible*. Also given that I don't spend that much time with her, when I'm with her I like to play with her and take her out and so on. But sometimes if I've just started to get into a piece of work, and she wakes up, I feel like saying, "Go away and leave me alone." I always thought I'd be too selfish to have a child. I suppose that worries me really, given that I judged myself like that in the past.

'I actually feel very distant from the women's movement. I don't really have a sense of it in the same way that I did in the 1970s. It's been interesting really, that for all the ideas of women supporting one another, that come having a baby you're actually on your own to sort it out as best you can. I've been quite lucky because of Jim's mum and Shirley, but it means that the extended family structure has been much more use to me than any sort of feminist network. In some ways I think it's created problems and difficulties with feminist friends. Some of them come down to just things like time, but others to much more complex things. I suppose in some ways I feel that most of my women friends made quite conscious decisions not to have children, so therefore I've stepped outside by having a child, so that in some ways there are tensions. The thing that bothers me is that I don't want just to be with women because they've got kids. I really don't want that at all. And that's probably what does happen. I don't like being seen as "Janie's mum"; it has resonances of "Ken's girlfriend", when I was 15 or 16.

In the baby club circle women introduce each other as
"Tommy's mum" or "Jessica's mum". And I'm not
"Janie's mum". I mean I am Janie's mum, but I'm not. . . .

'That's why work and political life become so
important, because just as I was saying about not being
identified as part of Jim, also Janie is of no significance
to people in the political context. They know I've got a
child, but when I go to meetings I'm seen as *me*, I'm not
seen as Janie's mother. It's been important to me that a
lot of the women I know who've had children have not
given up work or anything. I think without that it would
be more difficult, because you still feel the pressures, even
though you've got the sort of support that makes you feel
you're not a total lunatic. It's good to see people like
Harriet Harman, who's a feminist and an MP and a
mother, and GLC women like Deirdre Wood [the
councillor who caused a furore when she took her baby
into the council chamber].

'I'd much rather that Janie was in a creche. I still feel
that it's the best of what I could have at the moment. I
think that workplace creches don't actually help. It would
probably be the woman's workplace, so you'd have the
responsibility for taking the child there and picking her
up. I think community-based creches are much more
useful, because the thought of having to go to work every
day and take Janie and pick her up would be a total
limitation on what I could do. And extended hours would
help, because all the time I'm worried about getting back.

'I know of very few situations where women have
shared childcare where it's actually worked, because
people have moved away and things have happened. You
are in the whole legal thing of the mother being the
person that's recognised, and that gives you power. And
I don't really see that there's any way round that.

'I don't think that you can ever really imagine what it's
going to be like having a child. You know it all at the
level of theory, that there's going to be a child and it's

going to transform your life, but what it's really like has to be experienced. I'd anticipated the difficulties, but what I'd left out of the equation to some extent was the fact that you do enjoy it, and they are nice, and there are positive things about me being with a child.

'I'd say feminism has given me support in terms of feeling confident that it's OK for me to be doing what I'm doing – that is working and having a child – but I think in terms of direct help and support with that experience it hasn't given me very much at all. How I would manage as a single parent I just have no idea. But I was quite clear about that; there was no way I'd have had a child on my own.

'I think how I feel about my own mother is quite complicated, because it took me a long time to work out having an adult relationship with her. I had a relationship where I kept things from her and basically didn't discuss a lot. But what I've always had from my mother is a sense of being worth something, and I always experienced her as a strong personality. For example education. Although round where I lived the assumption always was that it was important that my brother passed the 11-plus and got a place at the grammar school, with me it didn't really matter because I was a girl. But I always had a sense from my mother that it was as important, and in some ways *more* important, for me. And that's hard to work out.

'It's sometimes difficult, because I definitely get a sense that my mother is proud of me, is glad that I've done well in her sort of terms, but all of that is, not undercut completely, but mediated by her regret that I'm not the sort of daughter she would have wanted – I've got funny ideas; she always defines me as "Mrs Pankhurst on her soapbox", so whenever I would be talking in adult company it's always, "Oh Mrs Pankhurst is at it again." I think she is probably quite ambivalent, because there's a whole load of things that she's really pleased about, but there's a whole other lot where she sort of wishes for what her friends have got — which is that their daughters live round the corner from her, they're married. She was actually quite upset when I was pregnant and that I did it knowingly. She could have forgiven me if it had been an accident. Interestingly enough, her biggest fear seemed to be that I didn't know what I was letting myself in for, having a child and not being married; how could I bugger up my life in that sort of way.

'There was an element of the stigma, but there was also a real fear for me, that I didn't know how horrible it was going to be, and how difficult, and that I'd got a nice little life carved out for myself, and wasn't I being silly. . . . She thought it would take a terrible toll on me, having a child. And she's actually quite right. And that really quite upset me.

'But I think she's been very important. She never really gave me support. It wasn't that. It's funny really, because she was actually a very strict sort of mother, and when I was an adolescent was very keen on how I shouldn't be allowed to stay out all night and that sort of thing. But when I went away from home to go to college she never encroached much on my life.

'She always had a job. When we were tiny she worked in a factory, and then she went to work full-time in an office. Which I can remember being presented as a big thing, as it was going to increase our money, and it meant I could have so much more pocket money. And we then had quite a lot of extra work to do. That's the other contradiction; for all she still expected me to do well, I was still expected to do the lion's share at home in a way that my brother wasn't. I feel that we're quite close in some ways, but at the same time there are a lot of families I know who are much more demonstrative about "I'm your mum, you're my daughter" sort of thing. It's not like that at all. Although we do speak to each other every week on the phone.

'I think the main thing is that she's actually quite a strong character. Presumably there are some elements of seeing in me what she couldn't become. She actually passed the 11-plus or whatever it was then, but it was never contemplated that you went on then. She wanted this commodity called education for me, but she didn't actually think through what it meant, and what effects it would have. Although at one level she must have done, because she was so clear about what I would do – much more than I was. I was never pushed, never ever pushed. I think this is the difference between the middle class and the working class – because they just feel that they're on the receiving end, they're not powerful in relation to all those institutions.'

J OAN RODNEY   Joan Rodney is 47, a mature student and single parent of a five-year old daughter. She also looks after her father, a semi-invalid. Smartly dressed and carefully made up, nothing in her appearance suggests such a demanding busy life.

'I was brought up in a very working-class area of Sheffield – rows and rows of back-to-back houses. My mother married quite late in life and she had had a child when she was young . . . and later she married my father. And she had a son when she was 40 and me when she was 42. A typical working-class family at that time: father went out to work, mother stayed at home. It was happy, except that my formative years were the war years. I don't know whether it was because of that that things came across very sharp, and being young and very impressionable things came across very sharply in a very political way. I didn't belong to a political family as such, but I remember very vividly the involvement of almost everybody in the area during the 1945 elections, and after we won the elections we had all this feeling of hope, that everything was going to be different. And this radicalism and all around in the streets. Plus the fact that I always seemed to think politically. I don't know why, but I suppose the very environment that I was brought up in. And I used to think why, why did people have big houses, when everybody I knew was crowded, particularly when people getting married were living with parents, and so that even overcrowded it more? I used to ask questions at a very young age, why did this exist? And then came the fuel crisis, and I can remember again, there being some very sharp issues in one's life. You know, of having to take the old pram round to the gas house, to the coke yard because that was the only source of fuel after our coal allocation. And everybody in the neighbourhood did this. And usually it were the kids that went anyway, but it was quite a jaunt to do that, to get a bob's worth of coal.

'So I grew up, went to a council school, failed my 11-plus, went to a secondary modern school, where they were concerned more with how we sat up straight. It was just the education that one gets because you're going to work in a factory. If you were quite bright at figures and writing then you'd be earmarked for an office job, but other than that it would be factory work. Mainly in Sheffield at that time, Bassetts the big sweet factory, Batchelor's the pea factory, a place called Compton's where they produced gravy salt – this was where the girls were concentrated, or engineering. I left school and tried a number of jobs . . . in the cutlery industry . . . various jobs I've done, all traditional female work. And then, I went into engineering at 18, into an engineering factory. I was very surprised when I went to work there because here there was a factory that had got organisation. I had worked in factories before where I'd been in the union (bakers' and confectioners', etc), but I was one on my own. But I went to work there and it

was organised, and the things that happened there, or
were not allowed to happen, were just a complete. . . .
From working in unorganised places, and jobs that were
just odd sod jobs, to going into a major industry and a
major factory that was very well organised was really
quite revealing. And I'd always been interested in the
trade union, and it wasn't long before I became a shop
steward. I was 20. And continued being a shop steward
until I left. I worked there for twenty-four years. It was
a section that was just for women. But I finally became a
convenor of the factory.

'So I was very involved, you see, in the trade union
movement. I had a space where I was always involved
with the shop stewards, involving shop stewards at factory
level, and a period of time out of that where I didn't get
so much involved in the meetings outside that, because,
as you can realise, there tend to be a whole lot of other
things that you wanted to do. You know you wanted to
be going out with other lasses dancing and so on, and
the workmates. And so I had about four or five years'
period where I was still a shop steward, still concerned
with problems in the factory, but not so involved in other
ways.

'I've *always* lived with my parents. I was brought up in
that age where young people didn't leave home unless
they got married. I didn't get married so I didn't leave
home.'

I asked whether she thought that being active as a trade
unionist and the time and commitment that that took up,
was a reason why she didn't get married.

'I don't really know the answer to that. I would now, I
would tell you now and say quite categorically that at
this moment in time I wouldn't get married. You
mentioned independence; I value that tremendously, for
all the things that I know about life, what a relationship

is, in a relationship, even living in one, would create, I wouldn't want. . . . But yes, I had all the aspirations that young girls have . . . that you're going to get married, and I wanted that I suppose, I went through that period just as much as the next lass. So there was never any inborn resistance to marriage, and as far as being active in the labour movement. . . . I really don't know. I mean women that are active in the movement meet men, single women that are active in the movement meet men and they get married to them, you know, but it just never seemed to . . . and I never felt that it was a conscious decision not to. . . . As I got older, more involved, more committed to what I was doing, then that idea of being married and having a family went. And then I became more conscious of my own identity, and even used to say, what I'm doing now I would never feel able to do. The whole period up to having Angela I had that way of thinking. I'd have never been able to do the things that I have done.

'I mean to be quite frank I was also brought up in — very much working-class values. What was underneath, you begin to question now; not only question, but you begin to wonder what were you doing . . . but nevertheless the working-class values of morality that I was brought up with were very strong. And whilst other lasses may have slept around or . . . I didn't. That was really sacrosanct. I was a virgin, and that was something to be protected.

'It was a working-class thing about women. I mean, men could do it, but women didn't. Don't forget that I spent my teens in the 1950s, when things were still rather austere in many ways. It was only when we got into the 1960s that certain things were being raised and so on, and as I say, what happened under cover . . . nevertheless that was the thing to be; not to sleep around, not to . . . that was something held very dear, this virginity thing. That was a very strong thing when I was in my teens. A very strong thing. And you know how everything's supposed to be tied up with one's sexual morality in an obsessively personal way – you know look at Cecil Parkinson . . . and it's all tied up with hypocrisy and all sorts of things. But you know, he could do anything, but let him step over the coals sexually. How can I explain it. On the shop floor you see, I had a leading position; and it was a position that was built up over quite a number of years: respect for oneself and, that you didn't sell anybody out . . . that you were a very responsible person as regards getting what the lads and lasses wanted, safeguarding, you know, their livelihood and so on. And I think along with that I must have always thought somehow, this thing of morality – that that was even tied up with it. So maybe that. Whilst I never consciously thought about independence, certainly that was tied up with it.

'As time went on I used to say; well I never go anywhere, only meetings. Who do I meet, what male do I meet? I think that has got an element of truth in it, because I just didn't mix with a lot of men, and mostly married anyway. But not in any other way but the agenda. Because that were important as well. I could never stand a situation where they were wanting to touch my arse. You were wanting to do a job of work in the movement, and them wanting to touch me arse. It was always a very strict – oh, you'd laugh and you'd joke – but they regarded me as Joan Rodney, just as serious a political animal as they were. Eventually, the thing goes around then, "Oh she must be queer" – because she wasn't sleeping with anybody. There's no slot she can fill. . . . If you're not married in this society, or you're not in bed, then you're either frigid or you're "queer" or . . . you know, you can't be *you*. But not wanting to do that, but wanting to do something else. Where I've always found great difficulty incidentally, in this, in this wanting to be, er, to *be* me, is to say, "Well I don't really think I am lesbian, I don't think I am, but just because – I think I'm heterosexual – but just because I'm heterosexual I don't want to be jumping into bed. So what!"

'I was in the YCL. Joined when I was 16. . . . A political party has got to be part of the people who constitute it, part of the life. You know, they come into a party, and no less the Communist Party, as human beings touched by society and all the values of . . . you know, they're not some kind of a super human being that with signing their name on a card rejected everything that society . . . even now.'

I asked whether it was in the 1960s that her ideas about marriage and sexual morality had gradually shifted.

'I'll tell you what it kind of leads up to, I'm convinced that things like that don't happen by just sitting down and thinking about it oneself. That's got to be prompted or touched by other factors, of what's going on in society. I started courting, I mean seriously, courting, when I was 25. You know the traditional courting, going to be married. Then he suddenly said that he was fed up and that were it. I would say that was a terrible traumatic experience I had, more traumatic than anything else in my life. Because here I was, you see, the man in my life, the one man in my life, that all the story books say, you know there it must follow the pattern of meeting somebody, courting, you know in the best traditional way, going to bed with him, and then . . . being rejected. Which really turned me inside out. For years actually. Well, there was nothing for about six or seven years, and then. . . . Well, it happened simply because . . . speaking frankly, I went to bed with him, but sex didn't mean a thing. It really did happen like "So what's all the fuss been about? So is that it then? Is that *it*? Is that *sex*?" So going without it didn't, I mean going without what – it didn't mean nowt, nowt were happening, and

I think thousands, millions of women are like that, get that experience, you know. So going without sex was bugger all, it hadn't started anything up inside me. And then, when I stopped thinking about marriage, and I mean when I really honestly stopped, inside me, not just saying it, not just saying I don't want to get married – actually I'd never said that in my life. But when I'd stopped wanting this thing that everybody does, that's when I began to really feel happy in myself. And to feel confident. I think I would be about, it would be . . . mm . . . not long before 30. You know, from 25, courting a couple of years, coming out of that terrible feeling. Not long before 30. In fact I'd say now that the most confident years of my life, when I really felt that I'd found myself, my own identity, was between 30 and 35. Really happy in myself because I felt so confident.

'My mother died nearly ten years ago, and my father's 80. He had a slight stroke last year, so I look after my father as well as looking after Angela. When I had Angela, because there's no back-up system or whatever, because I was literally on my own, except for my father, the first four months was extremely tiring, extremely, physically as well as mentally. Because you see I'd gone through all that period . . . found *me*, you know, enjoyed it. . . . I used to think, somebody up there really likes me, finally I'm out. I used to think how marvellous I'd escaped this thing marriage, and I hadn't got all those things like a husband who's traditional, you know "a woman's place in the home" and all this kind of business. I had at least escaped from all this. And I was able to do so much that I wanted to do and would never had had the chance.

'I was 42 when I had Angela. It wasn't a conscious decision to have her. Except that all single women are taking conscious decisions to have babies (in the sense that for them it's more of a choice than if you're married). When I say it wasn't a conscious decision, I mean I didn't just say, right, now I'll get into bed and

I'll try and conceive because the time has come for me to have a baby. On the other hand it was there; I think I must have thought if I want children, which, yes I thought OK, then, you know it's very, very late, there's not much time. And I'd got a relationship. I mean Angela was conceived out of what the agony columns call "a long-standing loving relationship". Well, so was mine. It had been a relationship for a few years. He was tied, lived in London, still does. No, there was no hassle. I knew the situation and I expected it, and it may seem, if I was telling the lass that worked on t' next machine to me this, but I'm not, I'm telling it you – she'd probably be very cynical about it and say, yes, that's what they all say. But really it didn't concern me, that he weren't going to marry me. In fact, I were glad it were that way. That's how it was, and I always *knew* that that's how it would be. That I was aware.'

I asked if she had been aware of how difficult it would be to bring Angela up on her own.

'I don't think that you're aware as much until you have them. . . . And so that independence, it's still there. Because there were so many things that even with a child, having all the difficulties of bringing up, of being a single parent in this society . . . that it's a selfish thing, of not wanting a bloke involved.

'Well, now I got Angela in day nursery . . . I couldn't get a job in engineering, tried a number of jobs. Of course I've got no formal skills, no educational background, the only thing I knew was engineering, could work on machines in engineering. Next thing was, well I suppose I could scrub a floor, so I went after cleaning jobs. But the hours in that were incompatible with Angela, by the time I'd have done messing about, and the money that they wanted to pay. So it was really by coincidence that I met a woman friend who suggested that I do a course, and I said can't see the use studying now. There are professionals – people who just spend their life doing courses and that. Because sometimes in the trade union movement, they're always at schools but never do nowt on shop floor. On no she said, so I thought I'd try, because I've got Angela in the place now, and I really want to do something with that time, something constructive . . . so I did a twelve months' course at a local college. It was called an 'A-level Alternative', not geared to A-level exams, but it was like an A-level syllabus. Then it was like circumstances that took me on the course to university; it was never any conscious decision, you know. From there they suggested oh, mature students are going on to university. Well I somehow thought when you heard about mature students – you see the advertisements and so on, and even for Open University – of mature people that had passed A-levels when they were young, but had somehow opted out.

'So I applied to Sheffield University and got a place, and you know, I'm over the moon about this, because then the whole thing had done like a twist and a circle of me being like confident and happy, and then this period of nothing and I was a nonentity, and the dramatic circumstances of having Angela, stuck in what I'd done all those years, took me on a course, opened a door that would never have been opened.'

I asked whether she had worked the year after Angela was born.

'I was on social. I was experiencing all the same experiences that millions of women do have when they get a baby, and they're in four walls with the baby. I were going through exactly the same experiences, I'm sure of it, of going to bed at night and I would cry and think, well, there's got to be something else; I am only 42, there really has got to be something else as well. You know, not just. You see you mentioned that you know, or know of, a number of women who have got into their late thirties and are actively taking decisions to have babies singly. But are they working-class?

'You know you've got all this cultural thing inside you, as well as everything else that you can't completely escape. All this background stuff, and there I was in four walls with a baby, first of all thinking, well, what do I do with this now? Lots of young women tell me that they have exactly the same experience. All this lovely thing during pregnancy, then they get and think, what am I supposed to do with it? And that's it . . . then, nappies, bottles, tired, and I don't think that was just because I was on my own though, but that was part . . . tired . . . then on to a clock, the bell rings, she starts crying, wants feeding. Well, plus the fact that you're on your own. You know, you've got no physical help.

'I won't say that I got a lot of emotional support, because you know sometimes people misjudge what you really feel inside. They think oh there's Joan Rodney, cool, collected, can cope. You know. "I admire her taking this decision to have this baby" . . . and it's not exactly like that. So I didn't get lots of emotional help, at all. Even from the women that I knew, because I think they got a misconception of what Joan Rodney was really like. Now after, as time went on a bit, I got . . . I mean like at this very moment, as I said somebody's been looking after Angela all day. That has enabled me to be out all day to go to a meeting. And that's marvellous. And I've got this kind of help all the time. They're party comrades. Women who are very supportive.'

I asked if she had had any involvement outside the Communist Party with the women's movement.

'No, not really. No in that sense, only I know some of the women who are feminists.'

Would she describe herself as a feminist?

'Yes, I do, and this is something that, well I think it's
sometimes misinterpreted, being a feminist. There's this
school of thought that unless you're bang on the line with
everything that is thought of to be radical feminist then
you're not a feminist. And I would contest that. I think
that the way I've fought for equal pay and got involved
in a dispute, stopping work, convincing them on the shop
floor that it would be the right thing for us to have equal
pay, showing them that they had to fight to get it and
needing that fight to get it – I consider myself a feminist.
All right, that's just one area, but it's a very basic area.
And convincing women that they've got to fight for it is
even more so than talking about it. It was in 1975. We
all sat in the canteen. We just clocked out. It was one
of those spontaneous organised actions. We clocked in at
7.30 and by 8.00 we were all clocking out and all went
to the canteen. We said, "We sit in here until we get an
agreement." We got an agreement by 11.00. That
happened. But it can take years really. Because when I
first went to work there in industry, to talk about equal
pay was a bit of a joke. When I think how radically that
moved. Twenty years *is* a long time, but how radically
that moved, from a position of at best a joke, and just
one or two people holding forth, and then actually taking
action.'

I asked how she had managed financially during the year
after Angela was born.

'With difficulty. I'd only ever had my wages, which was
spent, and always waiting for the end of the week. But
nevertheless, with a wage, well if I was skint I was skint,
there was always pay day next Friday. But when it came
down to social security, even more so because I lived with
my father and he was the householder – council house

in his name – and so you're considered as having not
much responsibility if you live with someone, and so you
get less, because you're only paying a little bit of rent and
towards heating etc. And in actual fact living with a
pensioner you've got more, and not only did I always feel
responsible, but as my parents got old, my my, there'a
a major contribution involved. Now when I had Angela,
I couldn't expect my father to take a drop in his standard
of life, which I'd kept – not in the lap of luxury, but a
bit more than other pensioners; not having to worry
about heat or things like that – my contribution. He can't
come down just because I'm having Angela . . . I even
said, and still do, that whenever I got a place in university,
and I got this grant, oh christ I hope I pass the exams –
because it's not the exams I'm worried about, or the
degree, it's the grant. Because the grant I get now, for
myself and for Angela, it's like a living wage. Well it's
like a wage anyway. I think I'm supposed to spend some
on books.

'Had I gone along and not had Angela, but been in that
position that I was telling you about. . . . I was on the
National Committee of my union, Women's Conference,
Women's TUC, District Committee – a prominent role,
more than any of the men, because I've got more
experience; some of the men were quite young anyway.
I took on board tremendous experience of the trade union
and labour movement and at Sheffield . . . that had I not
had Angela I think that the restrictions on that would still
have come up with the position that I found myself in
with my father. Looking after the aged parent is a scene
that's expected of women and there's no back-up system
from the social services. The woman does everything.
She's expected to cope and when one thinks – and it
really has come to my thinking more and more this past
twelve months – of the thousands of women that do
look after their aged parents, that give up lives to do that,
who've got no life at all. It's the saddest, you know it

really makes me sad. I think that I'm a political animal, to be able to see above it and rise above it. Yes, I've got all the problems that anybody has got about having to look after aged parents, but like I said I've got friends and I've got interests, that I am able to get to and so on. But when I think about the thousands of women that look after parents that are in far worse condition than my father, and literally give up lives in order to look after them and have got no back-up system. They're living on nowt and all.

'With single women of my age group the thing was not to leave home – maybe just a little bit less down south. There are single women of my age group whose parents are in their seventies now, getting infirm, many of them very infirm or helpless, then it's not only that they're expected, inferring that the outside world expects it, she expects it of herself.

'And not to do it would be . . . I think that it's something that I feel quite strong about, as far as the financial backing is concerned, because they lead an existence of economic deprivation, and I've always felt that if the women's movement is worth its salt then it's this kind of thing which it ought to get involved in. And I know the arguments. I don't accept them, I understand them though. The arguments are that if you get this, if you get back-ups and economic allowances, then you're perpetuating that it's a woman's job to do it. I've heard those arguments and I understand them. I don't really accept them. Because . . . nowt just happens, people make it happen, that has moulded society throughout history. And I firmly believe that if you venture on one struggle then it raises questions about so many other things. And if the movement really rallied to these kind of areas, like they do on abortion, then contrary to the idea that it would perpetuate women having to do this, it would raise the whole question of women having to do it.

'I'll give another instance today at meeting. Somebody was saying they'd read an article of somebody who was left, saying that people weren't so bad off, you know we still live in an affluent society. I think sometimes we tend to, I mean we mix socially and otherwise with people that are still quite affluent, still quite well off. I live in a very working-class area, very multiracial, West Indian and Pakistani. There's this young lass – who's white actually – got a couple of kids, typical working-class. Met her about five years ago and we always say hello and how are you when we meet. And I was in the Co-op getting a few things, in the food hall, and she were back of me, and she'd got one of these trolleys and it were chock full wi' grub, and I said to her, "God tho'll need that trolly to get up that hill." And she said, 'I don't smoke and I don't drink, but I have 20p on a round robin [accumulator bet] and I won £29, so I spent it all on grub." She'd spent it on grub for her kids. Now some women wouldn't know what I'm talking about. She was all chuffed because she'd got money to spend on grub. And I said, good luck to thee lass.

'I know other single parents . . . predominantly black. It seems to be part of the West Indian culture that a lass is going to have kids, and not necessarily married, and I live in an area where there's a large black population. Not my age groups of course, but younger.'

I asked whether she felt there was still a stigma.

'Well, I'd never personally felt anything at all like that, as maybe I would have done if I were 18. I told you that my mother had got a 15-year-old girl when she got married. The story that my mother told me – she was ready to cut her throat, dependent on what attitude her mother was going to take. She actually got the knife. Had her mother been the type of person . . . but she said, you'll have it and you'll live here and that's it. But that terrible feeling that must have existed. You see if I'd been 18 I would have had that; now the stigma never entered my mind, it just never was there. I went merrily along, and must have automatically thought that people – other women – would not think of it as being a stigma, but yet they might have done. Probably quite a number thought, oh poor lass, at the age of 42 a fallen woman. But I never experienced that from anybody.

'You see, my age group are grandmothers. And so in a sense they've got rid of certain inhibitions about the daughters. I don't think things are the same as they used to be. It used to be thought to be admirable for a mother to say to a daughter that had got pregnant, now only marry him if you really want to. It more happens that they might become pregnant, and there's more, oh well we're not getting married and that's acceptable. To the point where you get the reaction to it of people making right-wing reactions, of people making statements like it's almost an epidemic and girls are deliberately having them because they want to and they'll be well looked after by the state.

'To be a single parent is still a hard choice, and it's still among working-class girls, if they live in a family situation and the daughter has a child, the parents are still going to look after the daughter and the grandchild.

'Still the discrimination against single parents is still very bad. Not from attitudes, but from the structure of society. The cash business. It's ridiculous what they have to live on.

'I do think nursery facilities are really so basic it's unbelievable because in a single parent situation, talking about working-class areas, to be able to have a child in that situation, have a nursery that's purpose-built, and people that you've got confidence in, it was like suddenly taking a lead weight off the shoulders.'

CHAPTER 8

FLYING

In *Minor Characters*, her eloquent personal memoir of the Greenwich Village Beat era, Joyce Johnson recalls the first morning of a creative writing class at Barnard College, where she was a student. It's 1953. The distinguished-looking professor addresses his first question to the class.

> 'Well' – his tone is as dry as the crackers in the American cultural barrel – 'how many of you girls want to be writers?'
>
> He watches with sardonic amusement as one hand flies up confusedly, then another, till all fifteen are flapping. Here and there an engagement ring sparkles.
>
> The air is thick with the uneasiness of the girl students. Why is Professor X asking this? He knows his course is required of all creative writing majors.
>
> 'Well, I'm sorry to see this,' says Professor X, the Melville and Hawthorne expert. 'Very sorry. Because' – there's a steel glint in his cold eye – 'first of all, if you were going to be writers, you wouldn't be enrolled in this class. You wouldn't even be enrolled in school. You'd be hopping freight trains, riding through America'.[1]

The incident evokes the great imagined divide between male and female experience, male and female potentialities, and, in the Professor's brusque contempt, the vista of new creative freedoms in which women neither could, nor dared participate. They were, as Johnson says parodically, 'mere anonymous passengers on the big Greyhound bus of experience'.

At a distance of some twenty years from the appearance

of the Beat generation, her book disturbed these mythic components in its manufacture. With all the ironic insights of female memory and autobiography inserted into its masculine vision, and with its more mundane acts and gestures brought into close focus, the Beat myth and its heroes descend to a plane of reality that confounds the pronouncements of Professor X.

Not the least of the ironies is perhaps the best known: Kerouac, the literary emissary of male freedom from conformity and family life and its ties to women was also the boy who always went home to mother. And when he was far from home, it was women, Joyce Johnson among them, that he depended upon to smooth the rougher patches of life on the road.

Yet Kerouac's writing was, like the philosophy of the Existentialists in Paris, an early transcendental impulse in the momentum of the generation that endowed itself with the political will to change the world in the 1960s and 1970s, out of which came the women's movement. Across the years that intervened, multiple contradictions and conflicts of politics and philosophy erupted from a welter of difference: class and race, culture and ideology − and from that great male-female divide, both real and imaginary.

What is the most stubborn reality in the great divide between male and female experience, male and female potentialities? What makes it impossible for women as a sex to follow the same inclinations as men and go hopping freight? Is it the encumbrances of biology? Real or constructed, actual or historical? Is biology at the root of our subordination; not just the source of all the ills that female *flesh* is heir to, but of our social inheritance and its present consequences?

A complicated architecture of physical difference exists which historically has hampered women, and because of it women have suffered centuries of misery and ill-health, through childbirth, abortion, multiple pregnancies and dysfunctions or infections of the reproductive apparatus. Unspeakable pain, mutilation, crippling disease or premature death was many women's lot in the past as a result. It was only in the first quarter of this century that womankind began to be released from these horrors, with the advances of modern medicine, and more gradually with the introduction of widespread contraception, legal abortion, improved diet and more sanitary housing.

One way of viewing these changes is to see the gains made in women's health and life expectancy as a circumstantial precondition for both waves of feminism in this century, a view historian Edward Shorter tends to in conclusion to his painstaking and enlightening study *A History of Women's Bodies*.[2] Writers like Linda Gordon, Deirdre English and Barbara Ehrenreich[3] have uncovered the active historical part women have played in bringing these changes about, situating them in the context of women's struggles for access to contraception and safe abortion and for control of medical technology.

Female biology has been neither a curse of nature passively endured from which women were only to be saved by male scientific progress, nor wholly a victim of the latter. It is a mistake to see our bodies in themselves as the root cause of our social subordination, defining us in the first instance in a form that would give male culture an alibi for its hierarchies of weakness and strength and for separate spheres of female and male existence, the one in the home, the other out in the world. Our bodies have partly defined us in men's eyes, but they have also been defined, through the processes of medical technology, and through a mass of pseudo-scientific wisdom about the supposed limitations, frailties and defects of the female anatomy.

The nature/culture dichotomy was set up in the eighteenth century as the Enlightenment pushed forward its ideas of rational scientific progress, and women, already marginalised by property relations, and excluded from the central arenas of political and scientific activity, were identified with the 'primitive', 'natural' aspects of life while their domestic lore and knowledge of healing were equated with religious superstition or even witchcraft. Culture represented movement and progress, nature was eternally outside it, at the mercy of the elements and the cycles of the seasons. Yet culture was to act on nature, to tame it and control it. Culture signified the heights of human achievement, yet nature too was elevated, for its unspoiled virtues, its energy, its innocence and its association with the springs of human life. Placed in the realm of nature, women too were perceived in the light of these contradictory philosophical conceptions. But as the nineteenth century brought industrialisation and the new economic and class relationships created even wider separations between the male and female spheres, the distinctions and dichotomies were hardened. In the eyes of men, women were fated by their bodies – to fulfil a confined social role, to observe or be trapped by a strict sexual morality. The hysteric, physically and psychically paralysed by her socially restricted mobility, the tubercular young woman, cherished pale martyr of the Victorian age, the syphilis-ridden young prostitute – all cast their frail doomed shadows forward to our own escaping present, in which all of their particular bodily afflictions have been conquered, either by medical science or by the twentieth century's new ideas about sexuality and women's place in the world. But the prohibitions and restraints that bound them with such severity to their time have slid insinuatingly into ours.

Impossible and dangerous to fix the past in a single long imaginary stare, to stop it in its tracks when everything moves and frequently diverges from that illusory captured image. Victims stir and fight back, not wanting to be rescued at the appointed time when smooth segments of history meet and join. It's tempting to see ourselves as modern butterflies freed from the decaying chrysalis of oppressive physicality at the very moment when women shed those trailing skirts that gathered the mud and dust of the streets and cut the long mountain of hair held to be their crowning sexual glory when released from its combs and pins. (How handy a pin must have been, to a militant sufragette, or many a beleaguered woman . . . .)

Nature and culture: the dichotomy prevails, but with more

muted insistence, against countervailing evidence. The deceptions and ambiguities of nature, its many manipulations and constructions by culture, its estrangement from modern urban life. What remain are archetypes and abstractions, but potent ones, given material energy: woman earth-bound, maternal and stable; man reaching for mountains and stars, embodying the impulses of discovery and exploration, an insatiable curiosity. In painting and in statuary, woman is classically immobile, man in muscular movement. In advertising, blatantly and insidiously, women – or the feminine as an idea – are still nature to men's culture.[4] But more and more the conceptualisation of these dualities separating women and men are internally fragmented and contradictory. And what women have is a modern will to transcend them.

So what about hopping freight?

Joyce Johnson's memoir, besides illuminating hidden corners of the Beat experience, is also an instructive chronicle of a young women's coming of age in a social and historical context that restrained and subdued the impulses to excitement and adventure, in a woman. The Beats, in Kerouac's words, were 'mad to live'. Joyce Johnson, like a number of other young women who featured as minor characters on the Beat scene, was also infected with some of that madness. But her vision was framed by male expectations, her sense of direction muddled and distracted by male demands as well as all the intrusions of family circumstance. In the end she found it, as many women belatedly did in the decades that followed, and became a real writer – what she had aspired to ever since those early days in Greenwich Village.

The madness to live, the loosening of identity from its safe moorings in one place, and in one groove of life in order to let it find its way through a rush of new experience, is not a male prerogative. The urge to travel, to experience the elation of the rootless vagabond heading out towards the unknown, of the adventurer beating new paths, has always beat in the hearts of women too. To male chagrin. A man would prefer to set out on his own adventures secure in the knowledge that a woman is waiting at home in patient anticipation of his eventual return.

Female adventurers are few and far between in the annals of historical greatness, their existence acknowledged only in its footnotes and asides. In literature too, for almost the last two centuries, the female odyssey of adventure has been primarily an inner one.

Yet the image of the free woman, a utopian winged spirit unshackled by the chains of biology, is as vital as that of the female rootedness that claims autonomy in the inner realm of time and space. If women need 'a room of one's own' to concentrate their attention inwardly and guarantee areas of identity that belong to themselves and not just to others, they also need room to push outwards and extend experience and identity.

Flying offers the most vivid metaphor for this kind of freedom: unencumbered motion, travel, renewed discovery of self in circumstances that continually alter.

In the early days of aviation there were a number of women fliers as celebrated as their male counterparts for their audacity and achievement. Long-distance flights were public events bathed in an aura of glamour that gave their good-time heroes and heroines the status of film stars. Amy Johnson, the legendary British diva of the skies, became a national institution in the 1930s through her record-breaking achievements. But these, and her fame, were eclipsed by rapid technological advances and the advent of the Second World War, which made flying a serious business, too serious for women fliers to be given a prominent role.

Amy's story not only demonstrates the vicissitudes of the metaphorical high-flier in a world where men control admission, it also exemplifies the drama of a woman's struggle not to be grounded by the gravitational pull of marriage.

Anna Neagle starred in a bio-pic about Amy made during the Second World War as a vehicle for true Brit patriotism. In it we see Amy's pioneering solo flights across the world rewarded with international fame and official honours. Her public success is crowned with personal fulfilment when she marries another pioneer flier, the playboy Jim Mollison. For all his admiration of his wife's skills and achievements, Jim is somewhat put out when Amy announces her intention to continue flying – although of course the marriage hasn't affected his aviation plans. The issue is apparently resolved when they decide to fly together. But their first joint transatlantic flight ends in disaster; both are injured when the plane crashes after an error of judgment on Jim's part. Subsequent dual flights are beset with mishaps and failures, while Jim's philanderings and financial extravagances contribute to the decline of the marriage. It ends in divorce. When war breaks out Amy tries to enlist as a flier, but is turned down because the work is seen as too dangerous and demanding for women. She is finally recruited to the new women's flying corps that ferries supplies and equipment to the bases, at a safe distance from the combat zones. On one of these flights she meets her death in a fog over the south of England.

The contrast between Amy's solo success and the apparent impossibility of staying airborne on repeated married flights is inescapable. With a more deliberate irony, the low-budget short film *Amy!* made by independent film-makers Laura Mulvey and Peter Wollen in 1980 dramatises the split between the grounded flier, solitary by her fireside, now unemployable at what she does best, and the star whose epic flight to Australia in 1930 shared the headlines that made history all over the world. As Amy's route is plotted stage by stage on a map, a voice relays the daily chronicle of international events of which her flight is a part. Amy conquers space and time. But a woman whose single-handed actions hold the world's attention easily becomes a woman whose individual identity is nullified. She is the exceptional woman or she is nothing.

In the film *Christopher Strong*, directed by Dorothy Arzner, in 1933, at the height of Amy Johnson's fame, Katherine Hepburn plays an aviatrix caught in the impossible dilemma of career versus marriage. There is no resolution, and the film's ending is with her death when her plane crashes.

Flight represents freedom and liberation, a soaring escape from being earth-bound, from facing the unheroic realities of everyday life as a woman. The question of whether it is possible to reconcile an outwardly directed career that demands single-minded pursuit with the claims of a domestic relationship remains. Men can. Women are held back. But the possibility comes closer.

In my early twenties I seemed to be in perpetual motion: living in different countries, visiting others, a retrospective blur of ships, trains and planes. Travelling was like having wings, being in constant flight. I had no binding attachments, no children, nothing to keep me at a standstill. I went from Madrid to London, then gave up my job to live in Paris, returned a year later with a hiatus before Italy. Ten years ago I hitch-hiked across Europe, foolishly, alone, exposing myself to all kinds of hazards, but feeling invulnerable.

I couldn't settle down. This was no conscious rejection or escape from what it meant to be a woman, more a discontent with what the present offered, an unresolved sense of identity. Yet flight, travel I should say, has lingering attractions for me as precisely that. To be simply caught at the centre of movement, with time and space whirling by, would bring the giddy elation of wild possibility, of not knowing what lies ahead, of being lifted out of the continuum of work and domesticity.

Flight is heroism, the power to transcend destiny, the beating of wings towards utopia. It is all these things for women because women have forever been condemned to stay at home. In *Fear of Flying*, Erica Jong used it as a humorous metaphor for the sexual recklessness women seemed afraid of even at the height of the 'sexual revolution'.

If we are looking for daring and courageous heroines, we can find them. In the feminist rescue work of the last two decades, many of these have emerged from obscurity. Travellers, explorers, mountaineers, women revolutionaries, women who publicly defy sexual convention, scientists and inventors, women who have fought in national liberation struggles, women who have worked in war zones – all have been rediscovered and celebrated as proof of a spirit and capacity in women that equals and even excels that of men.

Their inspirational qualities are strikingly various. Some, either individually or collectively, have political meanings that enable us to see the past differently and make better sense of the present as a result – so uneven is the process of change and so elastic the act of historical memory. And history is written and rewritten in the light of changing knowledge and perceptions, but also of different ideologies.

Where such women exist for us in the here and now, as in the images of war and resistance that reach us in the pages of newspapers or on our television screens, they can, on occasion, suddenly lose the enormous cultural distance that divides them from us, and startle us into a recognition of acts and gestures we thought alien to our female 'nature'. It is most of all through the dislocation of war and the upheavals of revolution that women can cease to be contained by the definitions of femininity that a particular society might uphold. A society with emergency priorities, that has to divert its material and human resources into the effort of fighting an enemy, has less time for the conventions of gender or the cohesion of family arrangements. And the symbolic elements of an outwardly ordered world give way to a more unruly system of meanings.

There are cruel ironies in the knowledge that it can take a war for social organisation to be disrupted in ways that release women for a seemingly timeless bond of dependency and subordination to male initiative. The images of Arab women soldiers freed of their veiled passivity, of Central American revolutionaries whose air of disciplined confidence undercuts the macho ideal –these join the pictures we already have of the Second World War: the French resistance fighter, gun slung casually over her shoulder in the midst of welcoming crowds as the Allies enter Paris, the uniformed women on active service, the young women of the Red Army dancing in celebration with the American troops at the River Elbe, and before that the women defenders of the Spanish Republic.

All of these images have elusive and complex realities behind them. Under the alluring romanticism of combat for a just cause dwell histories of pain and violence, military hierarchies of power, and conflicts of ideology. In a world under nuclear threat and already encircled by 'small' military conflicts, peace has to be an ultimate goal, but some things have to be fought for. These combative and disruptive images move me and kindle optimism. Heroic women of action whose lives are disengaged from the knots of domesticity and maternity function as emblems rather than as models. They can give an imaginative undercurrent to our vision of female identity and our sense of its potentialities.

In childhood, such emblems of female heroism were rare. Those there were caught the imagination as cameos of fragile femininity pitted against a hostile or merely dirty environment. At 8 I was entranced by the story of Grace Darling in my school reading book — the lighthouse keeper's daughter who rowed through stormy seas to rescue, or was it to warn, the crew and passengers of an endangered ship. The twinned sweetness of her name lingers long after any clear memory of exactly what she did. Florence Nightingale, in a later reading book that featured several heroes of the British Empire, hovered, lamp in hand, a pious and demure angel of mercy, at the bedsides of sick soldiers, just as she still does on the £10 note. It was only a few years ago that this bland picture altered, as her feminism and the robust and single-minded character behind her achievements came to light in my reading.

In the Victorian period it is colonial women whose experiences, often overlooked in the long view of nineteenth century history, give us an unfolding panorama of female adventure. Any consideration of this is fraught with the knowledge of what colonialism has meant for the colonised. For women who took part in the exodus to the colonies it offered one of the few respectable outlets for adventurous impulses. I think of doughty middle-class missionaries, or lone eccentrics who braved the unknown with all the accoutrements of English decorum, importing its snobberies and absurdities to far-flung corners of the earth – some who supported the cause of independence fought for by those they encountered, others whose confidence in their own racial superiority was unmoved.

As well as the legendary chroniclers like Isabella Bird, Gertrude Bell or Edith Durham, travellers and explorers of note, there were many women driven to emigration by the stark limitations that circumscribed the lives of unmarried women of the not so wealthy middle class. The life of a governess was all that the majority of such women were equipped for outside the paternal home, and the economic realities that informed the drive to reform of women's education at home also contributed to the reasons for their departure overseas. Some were impelled by even more desperate circumstances. Working-class women from Britain and Ireland emigrated in their thousands to the unexplored territories of Western Australia. And there were the American frontierswomen, little celebrated in folk history, dominated as it is by cowboy buddyhood and the myths of masculinity under trial.

In the literary imagination, the nineteenth-century Gothic romances of George Sand and, dating from the end of the eighteenth century, those of Anne Radcliffe have offered accounts of female travel and wild adventure. The picaresque genre, its narrative of roguery grounded in more determinate and less fanciful social contexts, is seen as the province of the male hero. The assumption is that a woman cannot embark on such a course without her adventures being of an unfortunate sexual nature, because the apparent narrative drive of the genre sweeps its protagonist along an inevitably perilous path where he continually collides with circumstances and things happen *to* him, since he has no secure social foothold. And vulnerable women are sexual prey (witness female virtue remorselessly under trial in Richardson's *Clarissa* or Sade's *Justine*).

Yet the essence of the picaresque lies in the hero's ability to negotiate events, to overcome them and survive, while at the same time learning from his situation. By casting his fate to the winds he makes it a better one than if he had stayed at home. In this scheme of things identity must be transcendental, not rooted in virtue or fixed by nature.

Juliet Mitchell has analysed Defoe's novel *Moll Flanders* in terms of its heroine's relationship to early eighteenth-century society, what she describes as 'a period of turmoil during the establishment of the moral and legal basis of modern capitalist society' and 'one of profound value confusion and of unusual social, economic and moral mobility – the like of which has not been seen since in England'.[5] This confusion of values applies equally to women, for while Enlightenment philosophy was creating systems of value in which man exercised dominance, the growing spirit of radical individualism made no distinctions in theory between the *rights* of women and men. As Mitchell goes on, 'One of the revolutionary ideologies that went with capitalism was that all people were equal in the eyes of the Lord and this included the equality of men and women. Moll Flanders illustrates this concept but also the social reality that was always very different.' She sees Moll as 'a woman who is like a man in her economic ambitions and hence her independence'. She is capitalist woman at the heroic moment of capitalism.

Moll Flanders and other picaresque novels of the eighteenth century expressed the energy and mobility of a Europe at the beginnings of a new phase of history. With a few unnoteworthy exceptions that put a feminist gloss on the bodice-ripper genre of sexual adventures, it is a form that was not reclaimed by feminist writers of fiction, until recently. The 1970s saw the burgeoning of the autobiographical novel in intimate, confessional form, detailing the progression from pre-feminism to the dawning of self-knowledge, usually through the narrative of marriage and domesticity followed by separation and sometimes forays into lesbianism or the claiming of a lesbian identity – a realist transposition of what had in fact been the experience of many women in the women's movement.

That initially self-affirming phase of contemporary feminism has ended and many different kinds of fiction have emerged from the now rich and various strands known as 'women's writing'. But in the 1980s a small shift in the direction of a feminist picaresque can be detected. The most notable example is Angela Carter's *Nights at the Circus*. Angela Carter had already written a number of Gothic fantasies and was the best-known British exponent of the modern Gothic novel. But *Nights at the Circus*, although also exotic and rich in fantasy, is a new departure in its specificity of historical setting, at the close of the nineteenth century and the dawn of the twentieth. Accuracy of historical detail is not Carter's concern, but *history* is; the meaning and spirit of a time, a moment when the world is poised to enter a future that had all the possibility of 'hubris, imagination, desire'. These are the impulses that allow its heroine, Fevvers, to achieve the impossible: to fly. For Fevvers is the literal embodiment of that emblematic winged spirit, the New Woman, and, like Moll Flanders, a contradictory figure – soaring with all the possibility that the twentieth century will vouchsafe to women's freedom, yet with her feet firmly on the ground when it comes to matters of economic ambition. Fevvers, like Moll, is self-interested yet generous, unscrupulous yet kind, unfettered by a man, yet vulnerable both to the fatal predatory traps laid by powerful men and the more tender traps of sexual love. Like the rest of the novel's anarchic multitude, she is propelled in a rush of events and encounters, trials, dangers and discoveries, towards the future. Like Moll, she is capable of extricating herself from hazardous situations, by a combination of courage and ingenuity, charm and cunning. She endeavours to be mistress of her destiny, in head-on collision with what the constraints of biology and society may dictate.

This is a different kind of heroine from those of the 1970s feminist fiction. Where they can be viewed as victims at first imprisoned by, and then escaping from, the oppression of male institutions and the deformations of self-perceptions, to find a free though sometimes lonely identity elsewhere, here now is a survivor, resilient and ingenious, grappling at every turn with the contradictions of her world and forever in a process of becoming rather than resolving identity.

There have been other feminist fictions of the 1980s that cast their heroines within the same narrative form: Rosa Guy's *A Measure of Time*, also published in 1984, charts a black woman's experience from childhood in rural Alabama in the early years of this century, through Harlem in the 1920s, love affairs and motherhood, high living on the fruits of crime, then prison and poverty, to the stirrings of the Civil Rights movement and her son's new dreams. Frances Molloy's savagely witty *No Mate for the Magpie*, published in 1985, follows the life and times of a Catholic working-class child growing into womanhood in the north of Ireland, across the post-war decades, also engaging with a specific period in the history of a country and an oppressed minority within it. In lighter vein there has been Jill Tweedie's *Bliss*, one of several recent sagas of feminist adventure and travel. Director Susan Seidelman's funny and exuberant film *Desperately Seeking Susan* gave a picaresque form to the comic modernity of its plot. Frustrated young housewife Roberta leaves the stifling safety of suburbia to brave the hazards of the city in pursuit of the imperious Susan, swapping her dull identity for the daring fulfilment of her fantasies, after various unlikely mishaps and dangers through which the two heroines meet, outwit the villains and get their men – on their own terms.

All these refractory heroines echo something of a new confidence and a new awareness of uncertainties and contradictions. Women are not moral paragons, superior beings who only earn the right to claim independence on arrival at some definitive destination in the raising of consciousness. Change requires us to face the contradictory realities of what it means to be female in our time, rather than ignore them. This doesn't prevent us from aiming to transcend them, by crossing into the liberated zone of dreams and visions.

'One wonders if women still exist, if they will always exist, whether or not it is desirable that they should, what place they occupy in this world, what their place should be,' asked Simone de Beauvoir in *The Second Sex*.

There is no original state of female grace that we can return to and find a natural self, free of all social definitions. Whatever cultural or historical versions of femininity we inhabit are part of us, and in the sense Simone de Beauvoir intended, women still very much exist, in that, beyond biological distinctions, our humanity and potential is held to be separate, different, weaker and more limited than that of the male sex; the consequences are still devastating.

Of course it's our biology that visibly marks us out for this, so it becomes our problem, our encumbrance. We are compelled to struggle with its meanings, unlike men, who have no basic quarrel with the terms on which their bodies place them in the world, as the inheritors of human universality. Mankind doesn't have to interrogate its physicality, unless it happens to be female.

Paradoxically, the more we interrogate our femininity, and the more we decline to bow to its dictates, the more immoderately we are aware of it. By giving me a vocabulary through which I can speak of being a woman, discern its meanings everywhere, and turn a fine-tuned ear to them, feminism continually jogs my memory of difference.

Conventional language asserts the female as deviant or anomalous, through the assumption that the standard is male and women are absent from certain activities and occupations. Feminist discourse brings women insistently into visibility to compensate for this, and to remedy the wilful obscuring of women's achievements or the blithe failure to notice the value of things only women do. How to concentrate on the social differences between men and women, and illuminate their origins and inequities, without simultaneously intensifying the physical shapes of the meanings behind the words: man (no longer a neutral faceless image of *man*kind); woman (fleshed out in the mind's eye by her heightened presence)? Woman, women are everywhere; conjuring distinctly female creatures with breasts and rounded hips and menstruation – in perverse opposition to what was intended. It's wearying always to think of oneself as a woman, and to be perceived always as one is limiting, cutting off vast tracts of speculation and experience in which the sexual divide is less significant than other realities.

It's true that as women we continue to be affected by sexual difference, whether we bring it to the foreground of our consciousness or not. But we are not *only* women; the feminine identity mould is neither uniform nor seamless; sometimes we slide outside it into ambiguity. We don't stop being women; we forget we are. We become whatever else defines us. And this capacity for imaginative androgyny, to disregard our female biology and identify ourselves with divergent aspects of our work, our politics, our creativity, our relationships and even our sexuality, is a potential source of liberation. It gives us glimmerings of movement and change. Those women who have visibly traced their own transcendental arcs of experience – even with the dilemmas of femininity at their heels – are an inspiration that can propel the rest of us towards the future with greater confidence in our imaginary wings and the knowledge that the sky has no limits.

NOTES

Chapter 1
1   Jayne Anne Phillips, *Machine Dreams* (Faber, London, 1984).
2   Quoted by Crystal Eastman in *Equal Rights*, 13 June 1925, reprinted in Crystal Eastman, *On Women and Revolution*, edited by Blanche Wiesen Cook (Oxford University Press, New York, 1978).
3   Ruth Cavendish, *Women on the Line* (Routledge & Kegan Paul, London, 1982).
4   Llewelyn Davies (ed.), *Maternity: Letters from Working Women* (Virago, London, 1978); Cooperative Working Women, *Life As We Have Known It* (Virago, London, 1977).
5   Sue Sharpe, *Double Identity*, (Penguin, Harmondsworth, 1985).
6   *Women's Work in Deptford – The Double Shift*, published by Lewisham Women and Employment Project.

Chapter 2
1   Sigmund Freud, 'Female sexuality', in Pelican Freud Library, vol. 7 (Harmondsworth, Penguin, 1977).

Chapter 3
1   Adrienne Rich, *On Lies, Secrets and Silence*, (Virago, London, 1980).
2   *Women and Work: A Lifetime Perspective* (HMSO, London, 1984).
3   There's been something of a departure from women's magazines' role of moral and social mentor in several of the most recent newcomers to the market. *Elle*, launched in Britain in 1985, eschewed this role in favour of more fashion and showbiz – still dictating lifestyles, but at several removes from the cosy clubiness of old. Some of its established competitors shifted their accent in the same direction. The younger women's magazine scene has been transformed by the arrival of *Etcetera* and *Mizz*, also launched in 1985, and taking their cue from the success of *Just Seventeen*

(1983). These assume a readership that's sharp and streetwise, striving for style although on the impoverished margins of consumerism. All three credit their readers with more wits and intelligence than any of the longer-established teen magazines.
4   Deborah Gorham, *The Victorian Girl and the Feminine Ideal* (Croom Helm, Beckenham, 1982).
5   *Young People in the Eighties* (DES, London, 1983).

Chapter 4
1   See 'Wild nights', Cora Kaplan's incisive discussion of Mary Wollstonecraft's *A Vindication of the Rights of Women* and of Adrienne Rich's 'Compulsory heterosexuality and lesbian existence' in terms of feminism's own legacy of ideas about gendered sexuality and women's sexual pleasure, in *Formations of Pleasure* (Routledge & Kegan Paul, London, 1983).
2   Angela Neustatter, 'Cross dressing', *The Observer*, 3 November 1985.
3   Rosalind Coward, *Female Desire* (Granada, St. Alban's, 1984).
4   Jacqueline Sarsby, *Romantic Love and Society* (Penguin, Harmondsworth, 1983).

Chapter 5
1   Lynne Segal (ed.), *What Is To Be Done About the Family?* (Penguin, Harmondsworth, 1983).
2   Denise Riley, 'The force of circumstance', *Red Rag*, 9 June 1975; reprinted in *No Turning Back* edited by the Feminist Anthology Collective (Women's Press, London, 1981).

Chapter 6
1   Barbara Ehrenreich, *The Hearts of Men* (Pluto Press, London, 1983).

Chapter 7
1   Alice Schwarzer, *Simone de Beauvoir Today: Conversations 1972–1982* (Chatto & Windus, London, 1984).
2   Sheila Rowbotham, 'Hopes, dreams and dirty nappies', *Marxism Today*, December 1984.
3   The last administration of the Greater London Council (abolished in April 1986) was unique in making a policy commitment to just such an economic strategy, with Domestic Labour one strand in its short-lived Industry and Employment strategy.

Chapter 8

1   Joyce Johnson, *Minor Characters* (Pan (Picador), London, 1983).

2   Edward Shorter, *A History of Women's Bodies* (Penguin, Harmondsworth, 1984).

3   See Linda Gordon, *Woman's Body, Woman's Right* (Penguin, Harmondsworth, 1977), and Barbara Ehrenreich and Deirdre English, *For Her Own Good: 150 Years of the Experts' Advice to Women* (Pluto Press, London, 1977).

4   See Judith Williamson's *Decoding Advertisements* (Marion Boyars, London, 1978) for an analysis of how such dichotomies structure the rhetoric of advertising.

5   Juliet Mitchell, '*Moll Flanders*: The rise of capitalist woman', in *Women: The Longest Revolution* (Virago, London, 1984).